TORTURE
Justified or Unacceptable?

Erin L. McCoy and Lila Perl

Cavendish
Square

New York

Published in 2020 by Cavendish Square Publishing, LLC
243 5th Avenue, Suite 136, New York, NY 10016

Copyright © 2020 by Cavendish Square Publishing, LLC

First Edition

Cataloging-in-Publication Data

Names: Perl, Lila. | McCoy, Erin L.
Title: Torture: justified or unacceptable? / Lila Perl and Erin L. McCoy.
Description: New York : Cavendish Square Publishing, 2020. |
Series: Today's debates | Includes glossary and index.
Identifiers: ISBN 9781502644893 (pbk.) | ISBN 9781502644909
(library bound) | ISBN 9781502644916 (ebook)
Subjects: LCSH: Torture--Juvenile literature. | Torture--
Moral and ethical aspects--Juvenile literature.
Classification: LCC HV8593.P46 2020 | DDC 364.6/7--dc23

Editorial Director: David McNamara
Copy Editor: Michele Suchomel-Casey
Associate Art Director: Alan Sliwinski
Designer: Christina Shults
Production Coordinator: Karol Szymczuk
Photo Research: J8 Media

CONTENTS

INTRODUCTION

Torture can involve the infliction of unimaginable physical pain on another person. It might be done in order to extract information or to enact severe punishment. However, other forms of torture are designed to cause psychological or emotional pain.

British-born Muslim Moazzam Begg experienced this type of torture firsthand. He described forced nudity as among the worst treatment he experienced during his three years as a prisoner, held without charge by the US military in the Guantánamo Bay prison camp and in US air bases at Kandahar and Bagram in Afghanistan. Strip searches, defecating in public, and collective showers were required at Kandahar and Bagram. These

Opposite: A demonstrator reenacts the torture of a prisoner at the Abu Ghraib prison in Iraq in a 2006 protest in front of the White House in Washington, DC.

experiences were especially humiliating for the many Muslim prisoners there, who had learned from the holy book of Islam, the Quran, that nudity was an impure state.

"These were men who would never have appeared naked in front of anyone, except their wives; who had never removed their facial hair, except to clip their moustache or beard; who never used vulgarity, nor were likely to have had it used against them. I felt that everything I held sacred was being violated, and they must have felt the same," Begg wrote in his 2006 memoir, *Enemy Combatant: My Imprisonment at Guantánamo, Bagram, and Kandahar.*

"I would rather be killed than to be treated in this way," another inmate said of being forced to have his picture taken while he was naked.

The Impact of September 11, 2001

Why was Begg, along with hundreds of other Muslims, being designated as "suspicious," imprisoned without being charged, and then shipped—in February 2003, in Begg's case—to the American prison enclave called Guantánamo Bay on the island of Cuba?

Only some of the detainees were Afghans. Also among them were Pakistanis, Libyans, Egyptians, Sudanese, Syrians, Palestinians, and Yemenites. Many were Arabs, descendants of the early nomadic peoples of the Arabian Peninsula. All were Muslims, faithful to Islam, the religion founded in 622 CE by the prophet Muhammed.

The prisoners' initial incarcerations, wherever they took place, were often harsh. The Americans treated each captive as though he (very few were women) was a proven criminal, although no arrest warrants had been issued and no specific charges had been filed.

In Pakistan, where Moazzam Begg was kidnapped from his home at midnight in January 2002 by Pakistani agents, he was reportedly told, "The only reason we're doing this is because of the Americans ... If we don't, we'll be hit ... by President Bush's army." At US detention facilities, first at Kandahar and later at Bagram, Begg found that he had been labeled an enemy prisoner of war (EPOW), or an "enemy combatant." The crime of which Begg and others was suspected related to the world-shaking event that had taken place on September 11, 2001, four months before his arrest—the deadly air attack on the United States that came to be known as 9/11.

Early on that clear and pleasant Tuesday morning, four routine passenger flights had taken off from East Coast airports, two from Boston, one from Washington, DC, and one from Newark, New Jersey. Within roughly an hour, the two Boston-based flights crashed into New York City's World Trade Center, creating raging jet-fueled infernos of such intense heat that both of the 110-story twin towers completely collapsed.

The hijackers who had taken command of the flight out of Washington, DC, aimed the aircraft at the national military headquarters known as the Pentagon, in nearby Virginia; an explosion and fire did extensive damage to a sizable portion of the five-sided building. The fourth plane, out of Newark, appeared to be headed for the District of Columbia, perhaps to target the White House or the Capitol. But the passengers, who by then had heard of the other incidents, tried to gain control of the plane, which ultimately crashed in a Pennsylvania field.

In what way were detainees such as Begg presumably related to the horrendous deaths of nearly three thousand American civilians? The mastermind of 9/11, Osama bin Laden, who was part of a wealthy Saudi Arabian family, had begun planning hostile operations against the United States as far back as 1990. Bin Laden's animosity developed in part from the presence of

Rescue workers traverse the rubble of the World Trade Center on September 12, 2001, after a deadly terrorist attack. The United States government's response to these attacks included a military campaign that was later shown to include torture.

American army units on Saudi Arabian soil to train Saudi troops. This protective exercise of the United States was undertaken at the time of the first Gulf War (1990–1991), when Iraq invaded its oil-rich neighbor, Kuwait, and Saudi Arabia also appeared to be endangered.

To the deeply devout bin Laden, a group he defined collectively as the "infidel," or non-Muslim American troops, was defiling the birthplace of Islam and disrespecting its founder, the prophet Muhammed. When the Saudi government declined to expel the American troops, bin Laden fled with his family to Sudan and finally to Afghanistan, where he set up training camps for Islamic militants. There he built al-Qaeda, a powerful terror network, aimed at the United States and ready to strike Americans in various parts of the world as well as on US soil.

In Afghanistan, where bin Laden established his hidden headquarters in one of the most rugged and impenetrable landscapes on earth, he made common cause with an Afghan religious and warrior faction known as the Taliban. These Islamist extremists, believers in harsh punishments for those who defied the rules of the Quran, were seeking to take political control of Afghanistan in the wake of a ten-year occupation by the Soviet Union.

Torture and Antiterrorism

Following the attacks of 9/11, American authorities sought anyone who might have been associated with al-Qaeda or the Taliban. Once taken into custody, the detainees were subjected not only to physically and mentally oppressive living conditions but to a steady stream of interrogations designed to draw confessions from them at any price, including torture.

Upon arriving at Kandahar for the first of his two incarcerations in Afghanistan, Moazzam Begg was introduced to what was known as processing.

> *The noise was deafening: barking dogs, relentless verbal abuse, plane engines, electricity generators, and screams of pain from the other prisoners. Maybe I screamed too ... I was pinned to the ground ... and then I felt a cold, sharp metal object against my legs: they were using a knife to slice off all my clothes.*

What followed was a full-body, or cavity, search. Begg had been warned it might happen. Cameras flashed all around him. Begg's beard, another symbol of his Muslim identity, was shaved. His shackles were replaced so tightly around his hands and feet that he had to be half-carried to his windowless cell, where he was furnished with a bucket to be used as a toilet.

A year passed, first in Kandahar and later at Bagram, punctuated by interrogations that sought to obtain evidence that Begg had been involved in the 9/11 attacks. Shackled and hooded, Begg reports that he would be dragged to a room where military personnel and agents of the Federal Bureau of Investigation (FBI) and the Central Intelligence Agency (CIA) would prod him with questions. The topics ranged from whether Begg had ever contributed funds to al-Qaeda to whether he had been planning a suicide attack on Americans.

As a Briton, Begg was also visited during his time in Afghanistan by agents of MI5, the British military intelligence agency. Hopeful at first that his British citizenship would serve to prevent his being sent to Guantánamo, Begg was soon informed by his MI5 contact, "All I can tell you is that it's all in the hands of the Americans—they're calling the shots."

US Marines guard a new detainment facility at the Kandahar International Airport in Afghanistan on December 18, 2001.

It was understandable that fear, vulnerability, and anger gripped the American people and their government following 9/11. US territory had not been attacked since the Japanese surprise assault on the Pearl Harbor naval base in Hawaii on December 7, 1941. That event, which prompted American entry into World War II, had clearly been an act of war, and most of those who died were military personnel on active duty. But the 9/11 attacks had been an act of terrorism, defined by the FBI as "the unlawful use of force and violence against persons or property to intimidate or coerce a government, the civilian population, or any segment thereof, in furtherance of political or social objectives."

What did Osama bin Laden hope to accomplish in his campaign against the United States and the non-Muslim nations of the West? The leader of al-Qaeda interpreted the word *jihad*, or "struggle," in the Quran as "holy war" against nonbelievers. Bin Laden and his militant Islamist followers also believed that successful suicide bombers, such as the airplane hijackers that had destroyed the World Trade Center and damaged the Pentagon, would be rewarded in the heavenly garden of paradise for their martyrdom. Their sins would be forgiven, there would be salvation for seventy of their dearest family members, and they would enjoy the company of seventy-two young maidens.

Bin Laden would achieve his goal, he believed, through a series of actions that would strike the United States and show "the decline of the American government and the weakness of the American soldier." Nor, bin Laden stated, did it matter whether the terrorism victims were military personnel or civilians: "They are all targets."

After the 9/11 attacks, the United States was in shock. Some of the dead would not be identified for months, or even years. There were more than nineteen thousand body parts and fifty thousand personal items in the rubble on the site that would come to be known as Ground Zero.

What had gone wrong, and what was the United States going to do about it? Clearly, the immigration authorities should have scrutinized all applications for US visas more carefully to reveal possible connections with terrorist organizations. Some of the terrorists had even enrolled in US flight schools to prepare for piloting the suicide planes into their targets.

And what roles did the chief surveillance and intelligence agencies, the FBI and the CIA, take in tracking the origins and the designs of the attackers? Why, indeed, had the country been so lax in following up on previous attacks perpetrated by al-Qaeda? True, the al-Qaeda-linked perpetrator of a 1993 World Trade Center bombing was apprehended and sentenced to life imprisonment without parole. However, attempts to penetrate the bin Laden network in other "holy war" incursions had been half-hearted, based on poor intelligence, and generally unsuccessful.

All but four of the nineteen terrorists had been from oil-rich Saudi Arabia (with which the United States had friendly relations). However, the recently elected president, George W. Bush, chose to attack Afghanistan, the home base of Osama bin Laden and his Taliban hosts.

On October 7, 2001, the United States launched a long-distance air war on a land of harsh terrain, honeycombed with secret hideouts. The chances of finding Osama bin Laden and the well-hidden leader of the Taliban, Mullah Omar—even in a land war—were slim and would remain so for years.

Meanwhile, something else had to be done to fight terrorism. The intelligence agencies of the United States, especially the CIA—which was most concerned with foreign intelligence—had to be whipped into shape. The executive branch of the government, meanwhile, saw itself as an even better surveillance operative. Under the guidance of his vice president, Dick Cheney, President George W. Bush found himself conspiring for control of the nation's legislative branch of operations wherever individuals suspected of al-Qaeda activity were concerned. The White House was on its way to running an intelligence system of its own, choosing detainees, interrogating them on its own terms, and even employing harsh methods that fell under the description of torture to obtain answers to their questions.

As Cheney put it in a televised interview on *Meet the Press* on September 16, 2001, "We'll have to work sort of the dark side, if you will. We've got to spend time in the shadows in the intelligence world."

The detainment of people such as Begg without due process—fair treatment through access to a trial and other means of defending oneself—would become the law of the land for years following 9/11. Torture, meanwhile, would be used in counterterrorism efforts. Some saw it as necessary for the protection of the country. Others argued it was not only inhumane and unbefitting of the nation, but an ineffective means of obtaining reliable information. The debate over when torture is justifiable—if it ever is at all—rages on today.

Chapter One

TORTURE THROUGHOUT HISTORY

O n the international stage, all forms of torture were made illegal in 1948 when the United Nations General Assembly adopted the Universal Declaration of Human Rights, which the United States had helped to draft. The United States reasserted its commitment to end torture in 1994 when it ratified the UN Convention Against Torture and Other Cruel, Inhuman or Degrading Treatment or Punishment.

These efforts to outlaw torture, no matter the conflict, have come in response to a centuries-old practice. Torture has been used to a broad variety of ends throughout human history, and it does not yet seem that these multilateral efforts have been successful in ending the

Opposite: The iron maiden was a medieval torture instrument inside which detainees were enclosed and impaled on spikes.

practice. Let's take a look at how and why torture has been used throughout history.

Machines for Torture

The breaking wheel, the thumbscrew, the iron maiden, boiling oil, molten lead, the drowning chair for near-suffocation by immersion in water: all of these were instruments of torture used to inflict prolonged and unthinkable pain on a person.

On a pleasant day in the summer of 2001 (a month or two before the attacks of 9/11), visitors to the resort town of Atlantic City, New Jersey, ambled through an exhibit at the Tropicana Hotel titled "Torture Through the Ages." On display were instruments of torture from the Middle Ages, which had been used during the Crusades and the Inquisition, mainly between the 1100s and the 1500s. During that period, individuals suspected of being unfaithful to the Christian religion, or showing signs of doubt or disagreement, were subjected to a variety of tortures using objects made of heavy wood or metal, including racks, pulleys, chains, nails, and screws.

Racks were a means of suspending victims vertically until their arms pulled out of their sockets, or stretching them horizontally on rollers, until both arm and leg connections to the body were severed. The breaking wheel, or the so-called Catherine wheel, resembled a cart wheel but often had spikes projecting from the rim in a way designed to pierce the body of the strapped-down victim as it slowly revolved.

When a prisoner's hand was placed in the thumbscrew, the screw-down part of the device could be tightened enough to crush the thumb as well as each of the fingers, nails and all. Then there was the glove made of iron mesh, which was heated in glowing coals, then placed over the hand. There was the iron boot, too: with the victim's foot forced inside, torturers poured molten lead into the boot.

"That torture exists is a cruel and bizarre manifestation of the human condition," wrote Christine Farina in a review of the exhibit. "Torture is used as both a punitive and corrective measure, aiming primarily at the infliction of great pain. Severe pain marshaled, not in the pursuit of death, but as a means of 'dangling' the victim near death without the relief that death would bestow."

Many visitors to the exhibit stopped to gaze in horror at the so-called iron maiden. This standing box, shaped somewhat like a mummy's coffin, was lined with metal spikes. The design had first been used during the Ming dynasty in China. Once the victim was positioned in the limited space, the lid was fastened and the spikes punctured the body all over. How long did it take to die of bleeding wounds in the dark and airless embrace of the iron maiden?

Historical Reasons for Torture

The inflicted agonies of the past—and present—have always been an expression of power. Darius Rejali, professor of political science and author of the 2007 study on modern torture, *Torture and Democracy*, observes: "What's fascinating to people about torture is it gives one person absolute power over another, which is both alluring and corrupting." Torture, like slavery, Dr. Rejali notes, corrupts both individuals and society.

It is likely that, starting with the earliest days of humankind, there were not only examples of one-on-one torture but policies of torture carried out by public or state authorities. At certain times throughout history, the purpose of torture has been to obtain confessions from religious heretics and nonbelievers. Using torture to force admissions of regret and vows of repentance presumably permitted the victim to obtain a reprieve, in addition to satisfying the demands of the religious authorities.

Torture has also been carried out for political reasons. It has been used to obtain pivotal information about an enemy, to achieve revenge, to punish one's enemies, and to protect a nation's security.

Torture's immediate objective is not to kill. The death of the torture victim is, in fact, a failure on the part of the torturer because it ends the possibility of obtaining useful information, extracting a confession, or enacting long-term punishment. Unlike war, torture is also highly personal and this, too, is one of its agonies. As Dr. Rejali points out, "The people you're killing with a Predator [or other deadly attack missile] are not detained and helpless." An anonymous attack during wartime lacks the personal infliction of pain and humiliation that make torture all the more excruciating.

Ancient and Medieval Societies

One might think that only authoritarian states have permitted the practice of torture. This is not the case. In the democratic city-states of ancient Greece, where there were perhaps nearly as many slaves as citizens, it was legal to torture slaves and foreigners.

Greek democracy was based on laws reflecting the interests of the free citizenry, who were likely to own many slaves per family, including household servants. The concept of ownership of another human being was accepted. Infractions by slaves that were punishable with torture ranged from disobedience and petty theft to public dishonor and attempted escape.

Ancient Rome adopted a system of slave ownership similar to that of the Greeks, and similar methods of torture were used to extract confessions. As it was desirable that the punished slave return to work as soon as possible, forms of torture that would

Saint John (*front left*), a Christian martyr, was said to have been placed in a vat of boiling oil in Rome, but a miracle saved him from death.

not cause permanent disabilities were favored. Nevertheless, flogging with whips, rods, chains, and other implements was common, as was burning the flesh with red-hot metal or lacerating it with hooks that resembled giant cat claws. A less invasive but much-dreaded form of torture, also borrowed from the Greeks, was closely constricted confinement for long, unbroken periods of time in a body box that was known as a *mala mansio*, or "evil house."

After the fall of the civilizations of Greece and Rome, many aspects of their legal systems vanished. Later, in the Middle Ages, European societies were dominated by the powerful laws of the church, which sought out and punished heresy by means of inquisitions conducted in France, Italy, Germany, and Spain. It was during this period that the strappado, known as the "queen of torments," became the standard of torture.

Here is the strappado at work, as described by history professor Edward Peters:

> *The accused's hands were tied behind the back, attached to a rope which was thrown over a beam in the ceiling, and hauled into the air, there to hang for a period of time, then let down, then raised again. Sometimes weights were attached to the feet of the accused, therefore increasing the strain on the arm and back muscles ... Although torture was not supposed to maim or kill, a number of these methods ... surely resulted in permanent injury and disfigurement.*

As religious and governmental authorities were a united force in inquisitional matters, the judges who were present during the application of torture were also members of the clergy. Also present were a notary, a physician, and, of course, the torturer and his assistants. The accused, on the other hand, had no advocate— no lawyer, no witness. What's more, it was rare that he or she would have a means of appeal against the charges made or the punishment imposed.

Colonialism and the New World

The excesses of the Middle Ages eventually gave rise to more just and humane thinking about the cruelties of human torture in parts of Europe, such as England. The legal traditions of England, in turn, influenced the doctrines of human rights and freedoms written into the Constitution of the United States, which went into effect in 1789.

Nonetheless, the United States permitted the institution of slavery and punished slaves seen as disobedient in much the same way as the slave owners of ancient Greece and Rome had inflicted punishment. Once again, slaves had no rights under the laws of the nation. Native Americans, another marginalized group, were driven off their land with brutal tactics that often involved forms of torture.

Moreover, between the fifteenth and twentieth centuries, European nations such as England, Portugal, and Spain engaged in a vast program of colonization, sending their military, administrative, and economic envoys to regions in Africa, Asia, and the Americas. Under these powerful and exploitative European powers, torture was rampant. The humanitarian laws of colonialist nations, if they existed at all, fell away as rulers sought to build empires and untold wealth.

Spanish explorer Hernando de Soto and his men are depicted torturing the Native Americans who lived in modern-day Florida in their quest to find gold.

Torture in the Twentieth Century

Nor did the waning of the era of global colonialism in the early and mid-1900s signal an end to torture. The twentieth century, in fact, with its advanced technology and mightier-than-ever military power saw perhaps more human torture than ever before.

The tortures perpetrated by the Soviet and Nazi governments in the early to mid-1900s were not isolated events. Military dictators in Argentina, Chile, El Salvador, and other Latin American countries were responsible, during the 1960s through the 1980s, for the barbarous treatment of political opponents.

In Argentina, between 1976 and 1983, the right-wing military government rounded up students, trade unionists, left-wing activists, and numerous other suspects without arrest warrants. These persons, who became known as "the disappeared," were taken to centers where they were tortured until they revealed the names of other potential victims and then murdered, regardless of whether or not they had cooperated. To guarantee that there would not be an incriminatory body count of the thirty thousand citizens who vanished during the so-called Dirty War, the government of Argentina herded the doomed prisoners into airplanes and threw them—drugged, naked, and alive—into the estuary of the Río de la Plata, which flows into the Atlantic Ocean.

Notorious for having tortured and also murdered vast numbers of people were the Soviet Union and Nazi Germany. Their torture programs were part of extremist political, economic, and genocidal movements.

The Soviet Union

In 1917, as World War I (1914–1918) was drawing to a close, the nation of Russia underwent a massive revolution that transformed

A Torture Manual

As early as 1963 in the United States, the CIA published an interrogation manual offered as advisory material for governments in Latin America and elsewhere to aid in their persecution of political opponents. The 1963 manual and a second that followed in 1983 were known as KUBARK, a cryptonym for the CIA.

The KUBARK documents were classified, or secret, until 1997, when they were made public because a newspaper, the *Baltimore Sun*, threatened to sue the CIA under the Freedom of Information Act to gain access to them.

Many of the interrogative techniques recommended in KUBARK were said to have been derived from those used in the Soviet Union in the torture of alleged enemies of the state.

The US armed forces were also concerned with methods for withstanding torture, should members of the military be taken captive. To that end, a program called SERE (Survival, Evasion, Resistance, and Escape) was established in the 1950s. Its purpose was to train air crews and United States Army and Navy personnel to be physically and psychologically capable of dealing with imprisonment and torture. Many American servicemen had been subjected to torture during the Korean War (1950–1953) and the Vietnam War (1959–1975).

The KUBARK and SERE programs were familiar to Vice President Dick Cheney and the Office of Legal Counsel (OLC) at the time of the 9/11 attacks. These two programs affecting the United States' legal relationship with torture would influence the policies and practices of the CIA from 2001 to the final days of the Bush–Cheney administration in 2008.

it from a monarchy to a Communist country that in 1920 became known as the Soviet Union. During the Bolshevik Revolution, peasants, industrial workers, soldiers, intellectuals, and left-wing radicals rose up against their autocratic ruler, the czar. The entire royal family and members of the household were murdered.

A new government based on the "dictatorship of the proletariat [the worker]" was formed. A secret police agency known as the Cheka was established in order to seek out and round up wealthy landowners, members of the aristocracy, and other political opponents from various classes of society. Empowered by the state, the Cheka used brutal methods of torture to extract information from victims believed to be plotting against the new regime. The methods included "crowning" victims with barbed wire, which was tightened around the temples if an interrogation was not proceeding satisfactorily, and naked outdoor exposure to icy showers during freezing Russian winters. Between fifty thousand and five hundred thousand suspected political dissidents are believed to have died as a result of Chekist activity between 1918 and the early 1920s.

Even as the turmoil of the Bolshevik Revolution began to abate, the campaign to root out so-called enemies of the people continued under reorganized versions of the Cheka. A second round of major attacks on suspected political dissidents came during the rule of the Soviet dictator Joseph Stalin, who was determined to consolidate absolute power. The Stalin purges, as they were known, peaked in 1937–1938 and were aimed at farmers who had grown rich, professionals and intellectuals, army officers, and even members of the ruling Communist Party.

Torture was widely used. There were also events known as show trials at which the victims, who had already been publicly judged to be guilty, were exhibited in the courts. It is estimated that close to seven hundred thousand Soviet citizens were forced to make false confessions and executed, and at least eight hundred thousand were sent to prison and work camps in distant Siberia to starve, freeze, and die.

Nazi Germany

A major goal of the dictator Adolf Hitler was the "purification" of Germany through the destruction of its Jewish population, as well as the Romany people, physically and mentally disabled people, homosexuals, and opponents of the National Socialist (Nazi) regime. As a result of Hitler's conquest of surrounding European nations, he was able to have six million Jews and five million other civilians murdered between 1938 and 1945.

Many people arriving in the Nazi concentration camps were immediately executed in gas chambers, their bodies cremated in specially constructed ovens. But others were put to work and subjected to numerous forms of torture. Punishments were carried out and confessions extracted with lashes and whips, fierce dog attacks, electric currents applied to sensitive areas of the body, and strappado-like hangings. Standing cells were chambers for four people that measured 3 feet by 3 feet (1 meter by 1 meter) at the base. Prolonged confinement resulted in the deaths of all four victims. And hideous, deforming medical experiments were carried out on any man, woman, or child the Nazi doctors chose for the purpose.

Democratic governments, too, used methods of torture during the twentieth century. France practiced torture in the 1950s against people in its North African colony of Algeria, which sought independence. Britain used torture in the 1970s during the conflict in Northern Ireland. The United States, too, would utilize torture to achieve its ends. These methods would regain popularity and become more widely used in the counterterrorism efforts that followed the attacks of September 11, 2001.

As US general Dwight D. Eisenhower (*center*) looks on, occupants of a concentration camp in Gotha, Germany, demonstrate how the Nazis tortured them in this 1945 photo.

Chapter Two

A POST-9/11 WORLD

From the moment it became clear that the fierce and fiery plane crashes into the towers of the World Trade Center were aimed and purposeful, the White House knew that the safety and security of the United States were at stake. But what was the most effective way to fight back against an enemy force that was not officially allied with any of the world's governments, that could move swiftly and secretly across borders, and that was always gaining new recruits?

Military incursions in Afghanistan and, later, in Iraq sought to stem the growing influence of Islamist extremism and terrorist groups. However, because of the unique challenges involved in fighting such an elusive enemy, many US governmental and military

Opposite: Hijacked United Airlines Flight 175 crashes into the World Trade Center's south tower at 9:03 a.m. on September 11, 2001. The towers collapsed soon after, killing thousands.

leaders felt that torture was a necessary strategy for gaining key information.

From 2002 to 2008, techniques from the KUBARK manual on torture were utilized against terror suspects. Psychological torture would be embellished by physical torture, including slaps, kicks, dragging, walling, strappado, and waterboarding. Efforts were made by nonprofit organization Amnesty International as early as January 2002 to warn US secretary of defense Donald Rumsfeld that the hooding and blindfolding of detainees was a violation of United Nations policies on torture. The use of such methods would cause a great deal of controversy in the United States and around the world for years to come.

The Emergence of Torture

Shortly after the 9/11 attacks, the White House began drafting a plan to legitimize its treatment of the detainees caught in its web, treatment that was designed to extract incriminating information about prisoners' connections with al-Qaeda. The administration cast a wide net. No sooner had the United States launched its air war in Afghanistan in October 2001 than it began using low-flying planes to drop leaflets that offered bounty hunters rewards of $5,000 or more for the capture of suspected Islamist terrorists.

KUBARK provided a pattern for the interrogation techniques that would be used on the detainees who were rounded up after 9/11 and were immediately sent to American-run prison camps in Afghanistan and elsewhere abroad, as well as those who would begin to arrive at Guantánamo in January 2002.

Psychological torture was strongly suggested. It could be accomplished by making early-morning arrests, then blindfolding, stripping, and isolating the suspect. KUBARK recommended that normal eating and sleeping routines be ignored and that prisoners be held in dark, windowless, airless cells with minimal toilet facilities.

Stressful positions would also prove disorienting. According to KUBARK recommendations, the prisoner should be forced to stand for long periods of time while being interrogated. Restraints of other kinds should also be applied to cause discomfort. Exposure to extreme heat, cold, or moisture and prolonged sleep deprivation were also effective means of breaking down detainees' resistance to answering questions. Threats of pain were deemed to be more effective than the infliction of pain. What's more, telling the prisoner that harm would be done to his or her family was considered a useful way of extracting information.

While KUBARK outlined many of the coercive interrogation techniques that were used on detainees in the war against terror between 2001 and 2008, SERE advisers also counseled the CIA during that period. SERE training had for decades taught US military personnel how to withstand torture. Now, military advisers were introducing at Guantánamo some of the very torture techniques that SERE had been teaching its students to resist.

False Confessions

In various regions of Afghanistan, many of which lacked a strong central government, local warlords cashed in, using their private armies to round up prisoners for the United States. Notorious among Afghan bounty hunters was General Abdul Rashid Dostum, who delivered hundreds of suspects to the United States who in fact bore no evidence of guilt at the time of their arrest. One such suspect was Shafiq Rasul, a British-born Muslim of Pakistani parentage, who with two friends had traveled to Pakistan to attend a wedding and then had crossed the border into Afghanistan. The "Tipton Three," named after the town in England where they lived, were held in Kandahar and then in Guantánamo until 2004. Before they were released and returned to Britain, they were tortured to the point of making false confessions.

Captured in Afghanistan on November 28, 2001, and placed in shipping containers by Dostum, Shafiq Rasul and his two friends, Asif Iqbal and Rhuhel Ahmed, were eventually delivered to Kandahar Airport for transport to Guantánamo prison.

Their US captors, Rasul reported, did "[c]avity searches ... before they put us on to the plane, before they actually shackled us. And when we arrived at Guantánamo, they did it again ... just to humiliate us again." Before the trip, the three working-class youths had had their beards shaved. Dressed in orange prison uniforms, they had been marched stumbling and falling onto the plane, roped together, with sacks over their heads. On the plane, hands and feet shackled, wearing earmuffs, face masks, and gloves, they sat hunched on the floor, not permitted to straighten their legs during the lengthy flight in a cargo aircraft. No food was provided and no bathroom visits were allowed.

At Guantánamo, where they would spend two and a half years, Rasul was reportedly greeted by a guard with these words: "You killed my family in the towers, and now it's time to get you back ... [N]obody knows you're here ... and we could kill you at any moment." Interrogations lasting as long as fourteen hours took place in chambers where the men sat shackled and bolted to the floor. Strobe lights, loud music, and frigid air-conditioning added to their discomfort between questioning sessions.

Questions reportedly went as follows. "If you don't admit to being a member of al-Qaeda, if you don't admit to meeting Osama bin Laden ... if you don't care what happens to yourself, we can do whatever we want to your family, we can deport them back to their home countries, Pakistan, and the Pakistani government can do whatever they want."

The so-called Tipton Three—from left, Asif Iqbal, Rhuhel Ahmed, and Shafiq Rasul—appear at the 2006 premiere of *The Road to Guantánamo*, a docudrama about their experience being tortured.

In their cells, each of the three men was kept in isolation for months, during which time they were routinely beaten, subjected to temperatures of 100 degrees Fahrenheit (38 degrees Celsius) by day and icy air-conditioning at night with no blankets. Bright lights were used to induce sleep deprivation. Unable to pin any specific crimes on Rasul, Ahmed, and Iqbal, interrogators sought to determine whether they had appeared in a 2000 video with Osama bin Laden. Each young man was told that the other two had confessed. Without legal representation or any help from British officials, fearful for their lives and for their families, Rasul and the others confessed to having been in the bin Laden video.

It was not until their release was pending in 2004 that MI5, British military intelligence, looked into the validity of the confessions. Their passports revealed that all three young men had been in Tipton, England, throughout 2000. Their employment records proved that Rasul had been working in a video store at the time and the other two in a factory.

The experience of the Tipton Three led to a trial that reached the Supreme Court under the full name *Shafiq Rasul, et al., Petitioners v. George W. Bush, President of the United States, et al.* and came to be known as *Rasul v. Bush.* The group of petitioners included British, Australian, and Kuwaiti detainees.

On June 28, 2004, the court ruled 6–3 that, under the policies of the Bush-Cheney administration, foreign nationals were being imprisoned unconstitutionally. The Supreme Court concluded that, starting in late 2001, the White House had been violating the basic principle in American and English law known as habeas corpus. This Latin term refers to the requirement to produce the body (corpus) of a person who is being detained and is named in a legal document called a writ of habeas corpus so that he or she may be given a hearing in a court of law. White House lawyers had argued that habeas corpus rights applied only to detainees imprisoned on American soil. Although the Guantánamo base had been leased from Cuba indefinitely beginning in 1903, the White House asserted that the prison was on foreign soil. However, the court concluded that Guantánamo was indeed under US sovereignty.

The ruling decreed that the detainees had the right to challenge their imprisonment in an American court of law. It did not, however, require the automatic release of hundreds of other detainees held at Guantánamo.

The Geneva Conventions

The Geneva Conventions, first set down in the nineteenth century and updated in 1949 following World War II, outline the appropriate and acceptable treatment of prisoners of war (POWs). These standards of international law specify that wounded, sick, shipwrecked, and other POWs, whether military or civilian, are to receive medical treatment and humane care. The families of wounded and dead POWs are to be notified. Prisoners are not to be punished and are not to be sent to a third country for harsh treatment.

One hundred ninety-four countries, including the United States, signed the four Geneva Conventions, or treaties. Common Article Three specifically prohibits torture, which has been labeled a war crime under US law.

In January 2002, however, President George W. Bush came to the conclusion that the United States should abandon its adherence to the Geneva Conventions in dealing with enemy combatants considered to be terrorists. He called the historic documents dealing with prisoners of war "vague," and he accepted the judgment of the White House lawyers' memo addressed to him on January 25, 2002. "As you have said, the war against terrorism is a new kind of war [that] renders obsolete Geneva's strict limitations on questioning of enemy prisoners."

Who were the White House lawyers that Bush and Cheney had gathered around them from the very earliest days following 9/11? Known officially as the Office of Legal Counsel (OLC), and privately among its members as "the War Council," the group consisted of five men who were closely connected with the vice president.

In the fall of 2001, anger surrounding the al-Qaeda attacks was at its peak. Congress quickly gave the president the right to use "all necessary and appropriate force" to wage war against

The Geneva Conventions are signed at the United Nations in
Switzerland in 1949. The conventions define how prisoners and
noncombatants should be treated in times of war and prohibit torture.

any "nations, organizations, or persons" he determined had "planned, authorized, committed, or aided the terrorist attacks of September 11, 2001."

This granting of presidential emergency powers by Congress blocked legislative action against the White House for years to come. During Bush's two terms, ending in January 2009, foreign detainees on American or foreign soil would often be treated in ways that were illegal under domestic or international law. In addition, the US government would violate the rights of Americans suspected of terrorism by making "unreasonable searches and seizures" specifically prohibited by the Fourth Amendment of the Constitution. It would, in many people's opinions, violate the Fifth Amendment, which states, "No person shall be ... deprived of life, liberty, or property, without due process of law." It disregarded the Eighth Amendment prohibiting "cruel and unusual punishment" and the post–Civil War guarantee of "due process of law" to all persons born or naturalized in the United States, as enshrined in the Fourteenth Amendment.

Domestic spying in the form of illegal wiretaps and the interception of private e-mails without warrants was part of the secret surveillance of certain communications in, to, and from the United States. White House policy, meanwhile, paved the way for prisoner detention, treatment, and interrogation methods, including torture.

Defining Torture

Starting in 2002 and continuing into 2005, the OLC issued four memos that attempted to define what was and was not torture, even as a variety of interrogation techniques were being used on terrorism suspects. These memos, not released to the American public until April 2009 under the administration of President Barack Obama, became known as the "torture memos." Secrets

Setting an Example

On November 14, 2001, Vice President Dick Cheney declared that the Geneva Conventions would not apply to al-Qaeda suspects, stating that a terrorist does not "deserve to be treated as a prisoner of war." President Bush would soon follow the vice president's lead by ratifying that policy.

However, many argued that rejecting torture would protect US troops and American moral principles and would set an example on the international stage. In 2002, Secretary of State Colin Powell warned that opting out of the Geneva Conventions would "undermine the protections of the law of war for our troops."

Looking back at the United States' post-9/11 policies in 2011, Senator John McCain agreed that torturing America's prisoners endangers the lives of US military personnel, who might also be taken prisoner and subjected to the same tortures. McCain, who had himself been tortured as a POW, argued that torture is not only immoral but often produces "false and misleading information."

The United States, McCain concluded, must "stand as an example of a nation that holds an individual's human rights as superior to the will of the majority or the wishes of government."

In 2012, the American Bar Association's *Human Rights* magazine warned that the United States' decisions on whether to use torture could have a profound influence on the rest of the world:

> While there are many countries that fail to honor their pledge to eschew torture, none of them has the same power to unravel the fabric of the global norm that the United States—which has played such a leading role in establishing these norms—does. There is much more than short-term political point scoring—or even short-term security interests—at stake in this debate.

Vhat is water-boarding?

ater-boarding is a harsh interrogation method that simulates owning and near death; origins traced to the Spanish Inquisition.

bject strapped down

oth* held tightly over bject's face; water poured to cloth, over face

A uses ophane

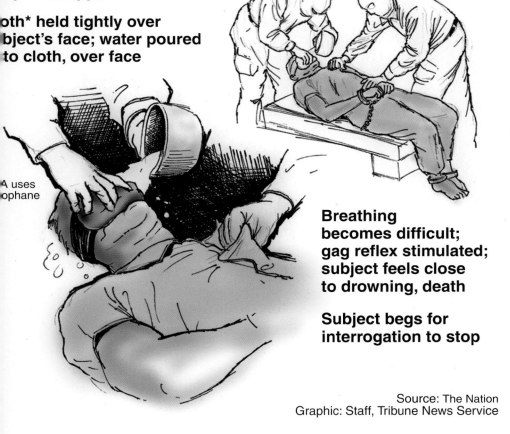

Breathing becomes difficult; gag reflex stimulated; subject feels close to drowning, death

Subject begs for interrogation to stop

Source: The Nation
Graphic: Staff, Tribune News Service

This graphic explains how waterboarding works. Some argue that waterboarding is a form of torture, while others insist that it isn't.

of the Bush-Cheney years and of their application of what many considered to be cruel and inhumane methods of interrogation were revealed.

What constituted torture? Were facial slaps, the collaring and bashing of a detainee against a wall ("walling"), forced shaving and nudity, and sexual humiliation forms of torture? What about confinement in a box only large enough to stand up in or only large enough to crouch in; the threat of confinement in a box with a stinging insect; and waterboarding? In one of the memos, dated August 1, 2002, the OLC considered these and other methods of imposing extreme stress on detainees. The OLC's goal was to outline how far prison guards and interrogators could go without technically inflicting torture according to the government's definition.

Waterboarding, a classic method of torture, is believed to have originated in the 1500s during the Spanish Inquisition. It simulates drowning and is continued until the victim indicates a readiness to cooperate with interrogators. As the prisoner lies face up, strapped to a flat board, water is poured either directly or through a cloth into his or her nose and mouth.

Richard Armitage, a deputy secretary of state from 2001 to 2005, chose to undergo the experience of waterboarding. In an interview given on January 8, 2008, Armitage reported, "A wet T-shirt or wet towel was put over my nose and mouth, and it was completely soaked. And then a question would be asked and I would not answer, and water would slowly be poured in this. And the next time I took a breath, I'd be drawing in water, whether I took it from my mouth or my nose. For me, it was simply a feeling of hopelessness."

Asked if he would describe waterboarding as torture, Armitage told the interviewer, "Absolutely ... There is no question in my mind—there's no question in any reasonable human being, there shouldn't be, that this is torture. I'm ashamed that we're even having this discussion."

Yet the torture memo of August 2002 did not conclude that any of the enhanced interrogation techniques it had reviewed were torture. In careful language, the authors of the memo—assistant and deputy assistant attorneys general Jay S. Bybee and John Yoo—wrote the following. For an "alternative procedure" to be considered torture, and thus illegal, it would have to cause pain of the sort "that would be associated with serious physical injury so severe that death, organ failure, or permanent damage resulting in a loss of significant body function will likely result." Also, to prosecute an interrogator for inflicting the described pain on a detainee, a court would have to prove "specific intent."

The memo submitted by Bybee and Yoo limited the number of days a prisoner could be deprived of sleep to eleven. It recommended having a doctor present at a waterboarding to perform, if necessary, an emergency tracheotomy. However, many argued that these precautions were not enough to prevent such acts as waterboarding from being forms of torture.

In essence, the 2002 torture memo gave the president sweeping power to conduct the war on terror. What's more, in the section he authored, Yoo stated that the country's ratification in 1994 of the United Nations Convention Against Torture and Other Cruel, Inhuman or Degrading Treatment or Punishment "could be considered unconstitutional because it would interfere with the president's power as commander in chief." The language relating to torture, which the United States had taken the lead in drafting in 1984, defines torture as "severe pain or suffering, whether physical or mental," and as "acts of cruel, inhumane, or degrading treatment."

Abu Zubaydah

On March 28, 2002, the CIA operating in Faisalabad, Pakistan, picked up the first person to be designated a high-level detainee, someone who had presumably been working closely with al-Qaeda for years. The man's name was Abu Zubaydah, a thirty-one-year-old Saudi-born man of Palestinian descent who had also been militarily involved fighting for Muslim causes with the Palestinians in Israel and against the Soviets in Afghanistan.

At the time of his capture, Zubaydah had been traveling with about twenty-five other suspected terrorists, men who had disguised themselves as women by donning burkas, garments that covered their faces and bodies. During the gunfight that preceded his arrest, Zubaydah jumped off a roof and was shot in the stomach, groin, and thigh. He bled profusely and for a time his survival appeared unlikely. Zubaydah's computer, cell phone, diary, and personal phone numbers were available to his captors. It was suspected that he possessed key information about the 9/11 attacks, Osama bin Laden, and the planning of future attacks.

So far in the war on terror, the White House had allowed the CIA to subject prisoners to solitary confinement in cells measuring roughly 6 feet by 8 feet (1.8 meters by 2.4 meters), extreme temperatures, blinding light, blasting music, threatening dogs, shackles, stress positions and beating, kicking, and dragging. However, these techniques, aimed at breaking down a detainee's resistance to interrogators' questions, did not succeed in extracting the vital information that White House lawyers felt Zubaydah and others must be hiding. They decided that harsher measures, so-called enhanced interrogation techniques, would have to be employed.

Following his capture in Pakistan in March 2002, Abu Zubaydah, the alleged senior lieutenant to Osama bin Laden, was flown to a secret CIA site in Thailand, one of at least eight "black

Abu Zubaydah, pictured here, was believed to be a senior lieutenant to Osama bin Laden, who orchestrated the 9/11 attacks. Zubaydah has been in US custody since 2002, during which time he has reportedly been waterboarded more than eighty times.

sites," or locations where highly classified defense or military projects (such as torture) are taking place. Other hidden prison enclaves outside the United States existed in Afghanistan, Egypt, and Jordan, elsewhere in the Middle East, the Far East, and eastern Europe.

Zubaydah, probably the most valuable suspect apprehended at the time, was believed to be third or fourth in command to bin Laden and the manager of a network of al-Qaeda training camps. Although he gave up information early in his imprisonment that led to the arrest of Khalid Sheikh Mohammed, the mastermind of the 9/11 attacks, the interrogators believed there was more Zubaydah could tell them. With the backing of the torture memo of August 2002, his treatment became increasingly harsh.

A Justice Department memo written in 2005 later revealed that the CIA had waterboarded Abu Zubaydah at least eighty-three times in August 2002. Additional aggressive interrogation techniques described by Zubaydah to the International Committee of the Red Cross (ICRC) were as follows. "I was taken out of my cell and one of the interrogators wrapped a towel around my neck; they then used it to swing me around and smash me repeatedly against the hard walls of the room."

Confinement in a small box, about 3 feet (0.9 meters) tall, was among the enhanced interrogation techniques approved by the August 2002 torture memo as "not torture."

"They placed a cloth or cover over the box to cut out all light and restrict my air supply. As it was not high enough even to sit upright, I had to crouch down. It was very difficult because … my wounds both in the leg and stomach became very painful … The wound on my leg began to open and started to bleed. I don't know how long I remained in the small box; I think I may have slept or maybe fainted."

Nearly four years later, upon arriving at Guantánamo in September 2006, Zubaydah reported to the ICRC that he had undergone ten or more of the abuses declared permissible by the 2002 torture memo. During his time at the black site in Thailand, the abuses that were not considered torture under the 2002 memo had ranged from facial slaps, walling, and stress positions to cramped confinement and near-suffocation by waterboarding.

Stress-inducing techniques continued to be applied at Guantánamo, even though it had reportedly become evident by 2006 that Zubaydah had little left to tell. According to press reports appearing in the waning years of the Bush administration (2007–2008), he had more likely been a "training camp personnel clerk who would arrange false documents and travel for jihadists, including Qaeda members," a "travel agent" rather than a high-level insider.

In 2010, it was recommended by the Guantánamo Review Task Force that Zubaydah face criminal prosecution. However, as of early 2019, Zubaydah remained at Guantánamo without having yet faced trial. He had been there for more than twelve years.

Chapter Three

TORTURE IN THE WAR ON TERROR

The horrible losses suffered by the American people on September 11, 2001, set off a campaign to find and punish those who had planned and perpetrated the attacks on the World Trade Center and the Pentagon and who had sought to carry out one more attack, thwarted by the passengers of United Airlines Flight 93, which crashed in a field in Pennsylvania. What came to be known as the war on terror would involve years-long conflicts in Afghanistan and Iraq and the tireless pursuit of suspected terrorists across international borders. In this new type of war, the question of whether terrorism suspects should be protected as prisoners of war under international law became a matter of heated debate. When it was revealed that many were

Opposite: Shortly after announcing the start of a bombing campaign in Afghanistan on October 7, 2001, President George W. Bush poses for photographers in the White House.

tortured and humiliated in facilities such as the Abu Ghraib prison in Iraq, international uproar ensued. Had torture succeeded in uncovering key information in the war on terror? And if so, could the ends justify the means?

War in Afghanistan

Speaking in full view of the wreckage of the World Trade Center in September 2001, President George W. Bush addressed his wounded nation: "I can hear you! The rest of the world hears you! And the people who knocked these buildings down will hear all of us soon!"

Although fifteen of the nineteen hijackers who had carried out the massive attacks of 9/11 were Saudi Arabian nationals, the target of the American response was Osama bin Laden, who was headquartered somewhere in Afghanistan. To that end, on October 7, 2001, the president ordered the first strike against al-Qaeda and the Taliban in the form of a long-distance air war.

Cruise missiles and military aircraft were launched over the rugged terrain of Afghanistan, where pinpointing secret hideouts in the mountainous terrain proved difficult if not impossible. Left to do the ground fighting were Afghan anti-Taliban forces known as the Northern Alliance, outnumbered at least three to one by Taliban fighters, who were supplied with guns, tanks, aircraft, and antiaircraft weapons by Osama bin Laden.

By the year 2018, the war in Afghanistan had come to be called, in some circles, a "forever war." Seventeen years after the war began, 2018 was projected to see more civilian deaths than ever. Afghan police and military forces, too, were dying in record numbers as the battle against Taliban insurgents continued. Meanwhile, a December 31, 2018, article in the *New York Times* reported that regional forces overseen by the CIA were carrying out torture and killing civilians, including children, sometimes with little or no evidence of their guilt. Some Afghan and American officials told the *New York Times* that these tactics were in fact pushing more people to sympathize with the Taliban.

Yet on February 16, 2002—only four months after the airstrike—a prematurely optimistic George Bush announced at a troop rally in Alaska, "The Taliban now knows what we mean. They're gone. And, guess what? People in Afghanistan don't miss them one bit."

Upon delivering his State of the Union message of January 29, 2002, the president introduced a new theme, declaring that "[s]tates like Iran, Iraq, and North Korea, and their terrorist allies, constitute an axis of evil, arming to threaten the peace of the world."

War in Iraq

Throughout 2002, as Afghan bounty hunters continued to turn in hundreds of persons they identified as terrorist suspects connected with the activities of al-Qaeda, George Bush began to focus on Iraq as the principal "axis of evil" nation. "Today in Iraq," he told the American people in a major speech in Cincinnati, Ohio, on October 7, 2002, "we see a threat whose outlines are far more clearly defined [than those of al-Qaeda]—and whose consequences could be far more deadly." The actions of Iraqi president Saddam Hussein, he continued, "have put us on notice—and there is no refuge from our responsibilities."

The idea of Iraq as an even greater threat to the United States than al-Qaeda was difficult for many to accept. Al-Qaeda had a history dating back to the early 1990s of declared enmity toward the United States and of highly destructive accompanying operations. True, Iraq was ruled by a ruthless dictator who had a record of immense cruelty toward his own people and who had in the Persian Gulf War (1990–1991) attempted to take over oil-rich Kuwait. However, Saddam Hussein was less fanatical than al-Qaeda in his interpretation of Islam. He did not preach jihad against the United States and, unlike bin Laden, he had not made overt threats toward Americans.

Even so, in a speech in October 2002, the president hammered home his reasons for believing that hesitating to strike at Iraq could put the United States in deep peril. "We cannot wait," said the nation's chief executive, "for the final proof—the smoking gun—that could come in the form of a mushroom cloud."

On March 19, 2003, President Bush announced the launch of Operation Iraqi Freedom and launched a massive aerial attack on Baghdad, Iraq's capital city. Initially the Bush administration declared that the war in Iraq was going well. On May 1, 2003, only six weeks into the operation, the president appeared on the flight deck of the aircraft carrier USS *Abraham Lincoln*. There, against a background that bore a huge banner reading "Mission Accomplished," the president saluted the carrier's crew in a ceremony that was showcased on television. In a speech that evening, Bush said, "The transition from dictatorship to democracy will take time but it is worth every effort."

How well was the invasion really going? In May 2003, Saddam Hussein and his top leadership were still at large in Iraq; Hussein would not be found and brought to trial until December of that year. Meanwhile, attacks by Iraqi insurgents against American ground troops were escalating week by week. Some of the attackers were members of Hussein's disbanded army or otherwise loyal to the former regime. Some were angrily reacting against the behavior of US soldiers, whose actions often offended the civilian population. The number of suicide bombings directed at the American military began to increase. A report by the International Committee of the Red Cross (ICRC) released in February 2004 described the actions of US soldiers as they investigated the sources of rebellion during 2003:

The Council of Ministers in Baghdad, Iraq, is engulfed in flames during the first wave of US attacks on March 21, 2003.

Arresting authorities entered houses usually after dark, breaking down doors, waking up residents roughly, yelling orders, forcing family members into one room under military guard while searching the rest of the house and further breaking doors, cabinets and other property.

They arrested suspects, tying their hands in the back with flexi-cuffs, hooding them, and taking them away. Sometimes they arrested all adult males present in a house, including elderly, handicapped or sick people … pushing people around, insulting, taking aim with rifles, punching and kicking and striking with rifles.

In the initial phase of the Iraq War, some 4,400 US troops would lose their lives and tens or possibly hundreds of thousands of Iraqi civilians would die. Hostilities would continue for seven years into 2009, when George Bush's second term expired. When Bush's successor, Barack Obama, took office, he began a phased troop withdrawal, officially ending the combat mission in Iraq on August 31, 2010. Some fifty thousand US troops would remain to "advise and train Iraqi security forces" until December 2011, as the country was still challenged by an unstable political alliance and limited public safety.

However, after US withdrawal, a new extremist group calling itself the Islamic State in Iraq and Syria (ISIS) emerged and began to claim territory. The United States launched airstrikes and maintained a military presence in the region in an attempt to hold back ISIS until December 2018, when US president Donald Trump announced the immediate withdrawal of the last two thousand US troops in Syria, against the advice of both US generals and his civilian advisers. ISIS, Trump insisted, had been vanquished. Less than two weeks later, President Trump revised his decision, declaring that the withdrawal would be carried out "slowly" and leaving the future presence of US troops in the Middle East uncertain.

Abuses at Abu Ghraib

The prison facility where many Iraqi suspects were lodged lay 20 miles (32 km) from Baghdad. It was a vast, grim fortress known as Abu Ghraib. Before the invasion, Saddam Hussein had incarcerated thieves, murderers, and political opponents there; the prison was notorious for torture and unreported deaths. The first US troops to take over found a number of blown-up buildings, destroyed sanitary facilities and kitchens, and rubble and debris everywhere as a result of mortar attacks and public looting.

In October 2003, soldiers of the 372nd Military Police Company of the US Army were put in charge of the everyday operation of the facility. Their own quarters were little better than the 6-by-10-ft (1.8-by-3-m) cells where the prisoners were

A US soldier appears to use a dog to scare a detainee at Abu Ghraib prison in Iraq in this undated photograph.

Weapons of Mass Destruction

Saddam Hussein, then-president of Iraq, is pictured in 2002. Hussein was accused of stockpiling dangerous weapons by US officials.

As justification for the proposed offensive against Iraq, the Bush administration alleged that Iraqi president Saddam Hussein had stockpiled chemical and biological weapons, poison gases, and anthrax. President Bush added that Hussein was seeking nuclear weapons by enriching uranium and could have a bomb capable of mass destruction in less than a year, at which time this technology could also be passed on to terrorists.

In the face of this evidence, on October 11, 2002, Congress approved the Iraq War Resolution, giving the president the authority to attack Iraq if Hussein refused to give up his weapons of mass destruction (WMDs) in accordance with a United Nations resolution.

Despite Iraq's denial that it possessed WMDs and its expressed willingness to allow the return of UN inspectors, a majority in Congress appeared to agree with Senator John McCain, Republican of Arizona, that the United States should move to attack "before Saddam can develop a more advanced arsenal."

During the first two years of fighting, as US troops, their British allies, and smaller military contingents from other nations penetrated Iraq, it was learned that Hussein had no threatening arsenal of chemical, biological, and nuclear weaponry. Nor had the Iraqi president ever had any meaningful ties with al-Qaeda, as Bush and Cheney had alleged.

In 2005, former secretary of state Colin Powell called his 2003 speech to the United Nations, in which he detailed Iraq's weapons program, a "blot" on his record. "There were some people in the intelligence community who knew at that time that some of these sources were not good, and shouldn't be relied upon, and they didn't speak up. That devastated me."

held. Everyone at Abu Ghraib lived on combat rations, known as MREs, or meals ready to eat. From the start of the US takeover, the prison was a target of insurgents. Mortars, rockets, and grenades were aimed at it day and night, but the military police (MPs) in the watchtowers were ordered to return fire only when they had visual contact with the attackers.

As combat units, the MPs were not trained to run prisons. Some members of the company had been corrections officers in civilian life. However, most had no idea how to deal with the large numbers of suspected Iraqi insurgents who were being brought in each day, sometimes with family members, including women and children. They were given few instructions other than the general directions of Lieutenant General Ricardo Sanchez, overall commander in Iraq.

On October 12, 2003, General Sanchez had signed a classified memorandum stating that interrogators at Abu Ghraib were to work with the military police guards to "manipulate an internee's emotions and weaknesses." He suggested taking control of the "lighting, heating … food, clothing, and shelter" of the internees. Similar suggestions for "breaking down" and "softening up" prisoners for "actionable intelligence" came from other upper-rank officers, including the commander of Abu Ghraib, Brigadier General Janis Karpinski.

During a visit to Abu Ghraib between October 9 and 12, 2003, a delegation of the ICRC found prisoners naked, painfully handcuffed, isolated in dark cells, roughly treated, and crudely threatened. When ICRC officials gave a report to General Karpinski about the conditions the delegation had witnessed, she wrote to them that "military necessity" required the isolation of prisoners of "significant intelligence value." Some time later, however, military intelligence officers in Iraq acknowledged to the ICRC that "between 70 percent and 90 percent of the persons deprived of their liberty … had been arrested by mistake."

Meanwhile, the detainees brought in to Abu Ghraib, regardless of whether or not they were believed to be of high intelligence value, continued to be subjected to physical abuse and extremes of humiliation. On January 21, 2004, a prisoner known as Detainee 07 described in a sworn statement to the *Washington Post* episodes that he said occurred between October and December 2003.

> *The first day they put me in a dark room and started hitting me in the head and stomach and legs. They made me raise my hands and sit on my knees . . . for four hours. Then the Interrogator came and he was looking at me while they were beating me. Then I stayed in this room for 5 days, naked ... [T]hey put handcuffs on my hand and they cuffed me high for 7 or 8 hours. And that caused a rupture to my right hand and I had a cut that was bleeding and had pus coming from it.*

Humiliation came in the form of enforced nakedness, of being made to bark like a dog and crawl on his stomach while guards were spitting and urinating on him, and of sexual taunting (by female as well as male MPs). Detainee 07 frequently referred to "the guy who wears glasses" as one of the perpetrators of his physical and emotional torture at Abu Ghraib.

"The guy who wears glasses, he put red woman's underwear over my head. And then he tied me to the window that is in the cell with my hands behind my back until I lost consciousness." The same guard forced Detainee 07 to lie on the floor on his stomach while "the guy who wore glasses" and others jumped onto his back from the bed. Following this, he was sexually assaulted with a baton. "And they were taking pictures of me during all these instances."

Who were the MPs responsible for assaulting the bodies, minds, and personal dignity of Abu Ghraib prisoners and taking photographs of these shameful scenes for their own entertainment?

"The guy who wears glasses" was Corporal Charles A. Graner Jr. Graner, who was thirty-four years old, had served in the Marines in the Persian Gulf War of 1990–1991. More recently, he had worked as a corrections officer in Pennsylvania. His army rank was actually below that of a military policeman, but he was put in charge of the night shift by Ivan Frederick, the sergeant in charge of the block to which he'd been assigned.

Upon arriving at Abu Ghraib, Graner became romantically involved with Private First Class Lynndie England, who worked as a clerk processing Iraqi prisoners as they were brought in, by the hundreds on some days. England had joined the army three years earlier at the age of seventeen, hoping to get tuition benefits for college.

The photographing of the prisoners is likely to have begun with Corporal Graner and Sergeant Frederick, known as Chip. Both had cameras. They were soon joined in their picture-taking by MP Sabrina Harman. "I remember the first day of working in Tier 1A and 1B," Harman said. "I guess the first thing that I noticed was this guy—he had underwear on his head, and he was handcuffed backwards to a window, and they were pretty much asking him questions. That's the first time I started taking photos."

Specialist Harman and her comrades took twenty-five or more photos that first night and continued for weeks to record prisoners, many of them naked and in stress positions, wearing hoods or women's underwear over their heads, being threatened by dogs, or piled up in a human pyramid. A corpse packed in ice, one of the two dozen or more detainees who died at Abu Ghraib, was photographed in detail.

When asked what the pictures were for, Specialist Harman said, "Just to show what was going on." But why did Harman choose to have Graner photograph her leaning over the corpse, smiling, eyes on the camera, and giving a thumbs-up sign?

Harman then photographed Graner with the corpse.

"I guess we weren't really thinking, Hey, this guy has family, or, Hey, this guy was just murdered," Harman later said. "It was just—Hey, it's a dead guy, it'd be cool to get a photo next to a dead person. I know it looks bad."

Lynndie England also appeared in pictures with the prisoners. In one photo, cigarette between her lips, she points at a naked, hooded detainee. In another, a man is lying on the floor with what looks like a leash around his neck. England, in her army fatigues, appears to be dragging him by the leash across the room. In fact, the "leash" was a tie-down strap for unruly prisoners. Graner had posed the photo to portray the detainee as though he were a captive animal.

On November 5, 2003, Harman took the photo that would become probably the best known and most reproduced after the Abu Ghraib secrets were revealed to the world. In a prank designed to stress out a new detainee, Sergeant Frederick ordered the prisoner to balance himself barefoot on a flimsy box that had contained combat rations. Frederick then attached electrical wires to the man's fingers and draped them over his chest and other parts of his body with the help of Harman and another MP.

The detainee, who understood English, was told that the wires were live and that if he fell off the box he would be electrocuted. Photos were then taken of the detainee, hooded and dressed in a poncho consisting of a blanket with a hole cut out for his head, his arms outstretched, and wires dangling from his fingers. The "mock-electrocution" victim remained posed for an unknown period of time, at least until Frederick and Harman had finished taking their pictures.

As frightening as death-threat experiences were for the detainees, the humiliation of being stripped naked in public, in front of both men and women, was even more damaging to the many devout Muslim men who were subjected to such treatment. Further humiliation was achieved by forcing the men to wear women's undcerwear on their heads. This latter tactic appears to have been a planned tactic, rather than entertainment improvised by the MPs. Indeed, the supply closet in the cell block was found to contain a large cardboard carton of freshly ordered pastel underwear.

The Prosecution of Interrogators

Sergeant Joseph M. Darby, a soldier in the 372nd Military Police Company, returned to Abu Ghraib from home leave in November 2003 and, curious about events that had taken place in his absence, decided to view some CDs Charles Graner had given him. Joe Darby was already familiar with the hooding of prisoners with women's underwear and the practice of hanging detainees by their wrists to extract confessions. But he was shocked when one of Graner's CDs revealed a pyramid of men's naked bodies photographed from behind. "I've been in the Army for eight years," Darby said, "and I've seen soldiers do some very strange things. So at first, I didn't even realize it was Iraqis."

On January 13, 2004, after weeks of indecision, Darby turned the photographs in to a member of the Criminal Investigation Division (CID). Graner, Frederick, England, Harmon, and three other MPs of the 372nd were suspended from duty and confined to their quarters.

Subsequently, beginning in May 2004, the seven soldiers would be court-martialed, sentenced to military prison, and dishonorably discharged. Two high-ranking officers were charged with lack of oversight and irresponsible behavior as prison administrators. Neither, however, received jail time or a dishonorable discharge.

Corporal Charles Graner was convicted of conspiracy to maltreat detainees, assault, indecency, abuse, cruelty, and obstruction of justice. He was dishonorably discharged and sentenced to ten years in military prison. Sergeant Ivan Frederick, the highest-ranking MP of the group of seven, was charged with prisoner abuse and torture. He was dishonorably discharged as well and sentenced to eight years in prison in 2004; in October 2007, he was released on parole. Private First Class Lynndie England, also dishonorably discharged, received a sentence of three years on counts

In a photo taken at Abu Ghraib in 2003, a detainee is shown with a bag over his head and wires attached to him.

of conspiracy, maltreatment, and committing an indecent act, but was paroled after serving 521 days. Specialist Sabrina Harman was sentenced to serve for six months and received a bad conduct discharge.

Brigadier General Janis Karpinski, who oversaw the detention facilities in Iraq (there were as many as fifteen such sites), was charged with dereliction of duty, misrepresentation to investigators, and failure to obey a lawful order. She said she had had no knowledge of the abuses at Abu Ghraib and that she had been denied entry to the prisoner-interrogation proceedings, further asserting that she was being made to serve as a scapegoat for higher-ranking officials. In May 2005, Karpinski was demoted to the rank of colonel and retired from duty. She was not sentenced to prison.

The only other officer investigated for the torture at Abu Ghraib was Colonel Thomas M. Pappas, who was in charge of military intelligence at the prison. His punishment for dereliction of duty, insufficient training of his military intelligence personnel, and improperly allowing the use of dogs to terrify prisoners, was forfeiture of $8,000 of his pay. Like Karpinski, Pappas served no prison time.

Public Reactions to Abu Ghraib

On April 28, 2004, the American public viewed the Abu Ghraib photographs for the first time on the CBS television program *60 Minutes II*. This revelation of the maltreatment of Iraqi suspects, four out of five of whom were later proved not guilty of any crime, was the first of many such reports. "Torture at Abu Ghraib," an article by Seymour Hersh accompanied by photographs, appeared in the May 10, 2004, issue of the *New Yorker* magazine. The released pictures, it was soon learned, were only a handful of the 280 or so taken mainly by Graner, Harman, and Frederick.

Most Americans reacted to the abuses that had taken place at Abu Ghraib with shock, horror, disgust, and embarrassment. It was easy, initially, to place the blame on the soldiers of the 372nd and to see them as "rogues acting out of their own individual perversity." Paul Wolfowitz, a deputy of Secretary of Defense Donald Rumsfeld, commented on May 4, 2004, "It's such a disservice to everyone else that a few bad apples can create some large problems for everybody."

At the same time, by photographing their own misdeeds at Abu Ghraib, the MPs had inadvertently launched an exposé that revealed the policies of their superiors. A stream of official documents—OLC recommendations, torture memos, and CIA procedures—rooted in White House policies made clear the manner in which the administration had chosen to fight terror. It seemed that President Bush was not being forthright when, following the Abu Ghraib exposé, he repeatedly stated, "We do not torture."

The immediate responsibility for the exposé lay with Sergeant Darby. The American public, for the most part, supported Darby's disclosure. He was lauded frequently on TV during 2004 and in 2005, he received the John F. Kennedy Profile in Courage Award. However, praise was not universal, especially among some members of the military.

In an interview aired on the CBS television program *60 Minutes* on December 10, 2006, Darby described his failed attempt to remain anonymous after he had turned in the pictures. Seen as a whistle-blower and a traitor by some of his fellow soldiers, he feared for his life and was returned to the United States, protected by bodyguards. Although many in his home community in Maryland supported him, other friends and neighbors shunned Darby and his family. Eventually the Darbys moved to an undisclosed location, where they were kept under protective military custody.

Yet, given the circumstances surrounding him in the fall of 2003 and early 2004, Darby stated that he would turn in the photos all over again. Asked by interviewer Anderson Cooper if it wasn't true that Saddam Hussein had done worse things to Iraqis when he was in power, Darby replied, "We're Americans, we're not Saddam. We hold ourselves to a higher standard. Our soldiers hold themselves to a higher standard."

Some military personnel would continue to insist that Darby, in being loyal to his principles, had been disloyal to his unit. Few people, though, would trivialize the events that had taken place at Abu Ghraib, as did conservative radio host Rush Limbaugh. Speaking on News Talk Radio 77 WABC, New York, on May 4, 2004, Limbaugh declared, "Somebody has to provide a little levity here. This is not as serious as everybody is making it out to be."

Limbaugh went on to make his case as follows. "This is no different than what happens at the Skull and Bones initiation,

Secretary of Defense Donald Rumsfeld (*center, in suit*) makes a surprise visit to the Abu Ghraib prison in Iraq in 2004 after a scandal over prisoner abuse shocked many around the world.

and we're going to ruin people's lives over it, and we're going to hamper our military effort, and then we are going to really hammer them because they had a good time. You know, these people are being fired at every day. I'm talking about people having a good time, these people, you ever heard of emotional release? You [ever] heard of need to blow some steam off?"

However, President Bush declared that what had happened at Abu Ghraib was "a stain on our country's honor and our country's reputation. I am sickened by what I saw and sickened that people got the wrong impression."

The Abu Ghraib prison was closed in March 2006 and was emptied of its occupants by August of that year. However, other military prison enclaves outside the United States, such as Kandahar and Bagram in Afghanistan, remained open.

Chapter Four

ENHANCED INTERROGATION AT CIA BLACK SITES

Even as interrogators from Abu Ghraib prison were being prosecuted for torturing detainees, enhanced interrogation tactics were still being used at CIA sites around the world. A 2014 report compiled by the US Senate Select Committee on Intelligence found that the CIA held 119 detainees at sites around the world between 2002 and 2008. Thirty-nine of those detainees were subjected to enhanced interrogation, which included waterboarding, exposure to extreme temperatures, and sleep deprivation. The committee also determined that twenty-six—more than one in five of the detainees—were held "wrongfully."

"The interrogations of CIA detainees were brutal and far worse than the CIA represented to

Opposite: The Salt Pit near Kabul, Afghanistan, a notorious CIA black site, is shown in this satellite image from 2014.

policymakers and others," the committee concluded, adding that the torture hadn't yielded meaningful results. "The use of the CIA's enhanced interrogation techniques was not an effective means of obtaining accurate information or gaining detainee cooperation."

Through a process known as extraordinary rendition, the CIA had long been involved in the practice of handing alleged enemy combatants over to foreign governments for incarceration and to obtain confessions. A partial list of participating governments ranged from Poland and Romania in Europe to Morocco and Egypt in Africa, to Jordan in the Middle East and Thailand in Southeast Asia. Since 2012, the nations of Poland, Macedonia, Lithuania, and Romania have been ordered to pay hundreds of thousands of dollars in damages to terror suspects whom they allowed to be tortured and abused by the CIA within their borders.

The secret prisons, or "black sites," where detainees were tortured seemed to operate without regard for US or international law. Let's take a look at what happened at these sites.

The Salt Pit

An abandoned brick factory north of Kabul, the capital of Afghanistan, was a CIA black site used to house suspected terrorists beginning in 2001. The CIA called it the Salt Pit. Detainees called it the "dark prison." In the facility's windowless cells, detainees reported being left to sleep naked on bare concrete, with only a bucket to use as a toilet. Guards reportedly carried torches and wore masks. Dr. Ghairat Baheer, one of the detainees, said US interrogators would sit on his stomach and left him hanging and naked for hours.

Baheer had been arrested alongside suspected militant Gul Rahman on October 29, 2002. On November 20, Rahman was found dead in his cell. At the direction of a CIA officer, Afghan guards had chained him, mostly naked, to the concrete floor of his unheated cell and left him there overnight. In the morning he was found dead of hypothermia.

Several years later, it was discovered that Rahman had been buried in an unmarked grave. No notification had been sent to his family, and the CIA officer who had ordered the fatal punishment had received a promotion.

A survivor of the Salt Pit who described his five months of imprisonment there was Khaled el-Masri, a German citizen born in Kuwait to Lebanese parents. Like many Muslims living in Germany, including some of the 9/11 hijackers, el-Masri participated in the religious and cultural activities of his local mosque. So even though he lived in Ulm in southern Germany, rather than Hamburg in the north where the hijackers met, he was initially confused with one of the terrorist operatives who had almost exactly the same name.

The el-Masri who was sent to the Salt Pit was an unemployed automobile salesman who had bought himself a cheap vacation package to Macedonia, a Balkan nation that had been part of Yugoslavia. On December 31, 2003, as el-Masri's tourist bus crossed the border into Macedonia, local authorities who had seen the young man's name on a terrorist watch list circulated by the United States placed him under arrest. CIA agents subsequently flew him, on a jet used for extraordinary renditions, to Kabul, where he would be jailed at the Salt Pit.

El-Masri reported being injected with drugs both before and during the flight. Since his cell in the Salt Pit had no bed, he had to sleep on the floor with an old blanket and an assortment of rags that he used for a pillow. The Afghan prison guards supplied his cell with foul-tasting, yellowish water to drink and allowed him three bathroom visits per day. "I really tried to drink some of that water, but it really stank. I could smell it from far away. I held my breath and took a sip. But the aftertaste stayed for more than an hour," he recalls. Because combat rations were not available, el-Masri was fed a sparse diet of food that brought on bouts of diarrhea.

El-Masri had been beaten repeatedly upon being arrested in Macedonia. When he arrived at the Salt Pit, he was placed in chains and painfully dragged to interrogations with his arms locked above his head. When he repeatedly denied knowing any of the hijackers of 9/11, he was accused of being uncooperative. "You are here in a country without law," his interrogator told him, "and no one knows where you are. Do you know what that means?"

In protest, el-Masri went on a hunger strike, holding out for thirty-seven days until he was force-fed by masked men who put a tube down his nose into his stomach to introduce liquid food.

CIA officials soon realized that if el-Masri, a German citizen, died while in American custody, the Salt Pit and other secret prisons could face global scrutiny. It also became clear that el-Masri's arrest had been a case of mistaken identity. He was ordered to be released by the highest CIA authority: the agency's director, George Tenet. No CIA operative was held responsible for the error or for the treatment of el-Masri.

On May 28, 2004, five months after his arrest in Macedonia, el-Masri was surreptitiously returned to Germany. His jailers had first put him on a more nourishing diet to bolster his health and restore some of the weight he had lost at the Salt Pit. This didn't work; el-Masri had lost 60 pounds (27 kilograms). A CIA executive jet then flew him to Albania, where he was transferred onto a commercial flight to Germany.

The story of el-Masri's kidnapping was soon made public, and he was interviewed by ZDF television in Germany. Important details of his experience were verified through police investigations and the flight logs of the CIA rendition jets. US secretary of state Condoleezza Rice attempted to quell public outrage in Germany and elsewhere in Europe by offering the assurance, in

Khaled el-Masri, a German citizen, discusses his wrongful captivity and subsequent torture after a court date in the United States in 2006. The court case accused the CIA director of violating human rights laws in its use of torture. The case was dismissed.

a 2005 statement, that "[i]f mistakes have been made, they are always corrected rapidly."

In 2006, the American Civil Liberties Union (ACLU) filed a lawsuit against George Tenet on behalf of el-Masri. The suit, *El-Masri v. Tenet*, charged that the CIA director had violated the human rights laws of the United States and other nations when it subjected el-Masri to torture in Macedonia and the Salt Pit and when it held him incommunicado in Afghanistan after authorities had learned that he had been wrongfully imprisoned. The corporations that owned the executive jets used for the rendition were also sued.

However, in May 2006, a lower federal court dismissed the case and, in March 2007, a federal appeals court declined to hear the case. Both courts cited the risk of revealing "state secrets." In October 2007, the US Supreme Court refused to hear the el-Masri case, without comment, allowing the lower court's ruling to stand. Many observers of the case could only conclude that the courts were protecting the secret of the administration's foreign prison sites.

In 2008, the ACLU brought the former detainee to the United States to enter a plea for a hearing of *El-Masri v. Tenet*. In a speech in Washington, DC, el-Masri said, "[The United States] is not democracy. In my opinion, this is how you establish a dictatorial regime. Countries are occupied, people are killed, and we cannot say anything because it's all considered a state secret."

In 2012, the European Court of Human Rights handed down a different ruling. It found that Macedonia had violated el-Masri's rights by handing him over into US custody. It ordered that Macedonia pay el-Masri compensation.

"This is the first court to comprehensively and specifically find that the CIA's rendition techniques amounted to torture," wrote Amrit Singh, a senior legal officer at the Open Society Justice Initiative, in an op-ed for the *Guardian* newspaper. "The

Rendition, Torture, and a False Confession

On September 26, 2002, Maher Arar, a Syrian-born Canadian citizen returning home from vacation, suddenly found himself under arrest at John F. Kennedy International Airport in New York City. He was refused a phone call and a lawyer and was repeatedly asked about a man named Abdullah Almaki, another Syrian-born Canadian, whose name appeared as a witness on a rental lease that Arar signed in 1997. Almaki was suspected of belonging to al-Qaeda.

Arar explained that Almaki was an acquaintance whom he didn't know very well. After long hours of interrogation, Arar was given one opportunity to notify his family and obtain a lawyer, but his lawyer soon lost access to him. He was transported to Syria. On October 9, he was taken to his tiny, dark cell.

During his time in prison, Arar was repeatedly beaten on the palms, wrists, and other parts of his body with a shredded black electrical cable. The Syrians beat him so badly that he confessed to having received military training in Afghanistan even though he had never been there.

Because of the efforts of Arar's wife to publicize the situation, he began to receive visits from the Canadian consul as early as October 2002. In April, he met the Canadian ambassador. Finally, on October 5, 2003, more than a year after his arrest, he was released and flown home to Canada.

In 2004, Arar filed a lawsuit against the US government, but the suit proved unsuccessful, and he remains on a US terrorist watch list. As in the case of Khaled el-Masri, the courts dismissed or rejected *Arar v. Ashcroft, et al.* to protect state secrets. The Canadian government, however, awarded Arar $10.5 million in damages for his wrongful arrest and the violation of his civil, international, and human rights.

decision stands in sharp contrast to the abject failure of US courts to deliver justice to victims of US torture and rendition."

High-Value Detainees

March 28, 2002, saw the capture Abu Zubaydah, the first of the so-called high-value detainees that the United States had been seeking since September 2001. Based on evidence found among the personal items found in his possession—his computer, cell phone, diary, and personal phone numbers—he was believed to have strong ties to Osama bin Laden.

With the goal of extracting the maximum amount of information from Zubaydah and other detainees expected to come into custody, the White House had its lawyers draft the document now known as the torture memo of August 1, 2002. The memo was aimed at assessing the techniques already in use—shackling, beating, slapping, shaking, walling, immobilizing for long periods, sleep deprivation, exposure to extremes of temperature, and personal and racial humiliation.

According to the memo, techniques such as shackling, beating, slapping, and sleep deprivation, which were being employed at Guantánamo, were not torture. As stated earlier, torture required suffering "equivalent in intensity to the pain accompanying serious physical injury, such as organ failure, impairment of bodily function, or even death."

What about waterboarding, a technique as old as the Spanish Inquisition of the 1500s? As far as is known, waterboarding was never used at Guantánamo, which was open to visits from members of the American military and the International Committee of the Red Cross. However, there was another place it could be used: at the CIA black sites in nations that not only habitually employed torture but also had economic and political reasons to court the goodwill of the United States.

The eighty-three waterboardings of Abu Zubaydah are believed to have taken place at a black site in Thailand. The CIA taped the procedure, perhaps to protect the agency in the event of the death of the man who was then its key witness. However, a growing number of requests for the tapes by courts and investigative bodies led to their destruction by the CIA in 2005 at the order of the agency's Clandestine Services unit.

According to Zubaydah's report to the Red Cross, "the CIA waterboarded him at least ten times in a single week, often twice a day. On one day, he claimed, he was waterboarded three times." He described being strapped down to a hard surface with leather fastenings, his feet elevated, and water being poured into his nose and mouth simultaneously, bringing on gagging, regurgitating, and the terrifying sensation of drowning.

Khalid Sheikh Mohammed

It is uncertain when, during his interrogations, Zubaydah gave up the name of the man who would later confess to being the mastermind of the 9/11 attacks, Khalid Sheikh Mohammed. Whether it came up during a waterboarding session is unclear. In view of what was documented on Zubaydah's computer, diary, and other possessions at the time of his capture, it's not unlikely that Mohammed's name came to light immediately. Even so, this high-level al-Qaeda operative was not unknown to the FBI, which had been seeking him since 1993.

When the 9/11 suspect was finally taken into US custody at four o'clock in the morning on March 1, 2003, in Rawalpindi, Pakistan, his capture was the direct result of a payment of $25 million by the American government to an informant in Pakistan.

Previously, the prisoner had been photographed as resembling a solemn black-bearded cleric. The image of Khalid Sheikh

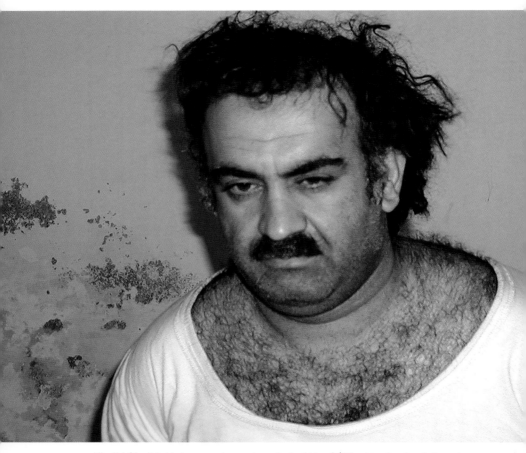

Khalid Sheikh Mohammed, mastermind of the 9/11 attacks, is pictured on March 1, 2003, shortly after he was captured by US forces.

Mohammed that was flashed around the world in early March 2003, however, showed an unkempt man in a rumpled undershirt, with short matted hair and no beard. The top-value al-Qaeda operative then disappeared from the limelight to be whisked away to various black site prisons. The one in which he spent the most time is believed to have been in Poland.

In reports to the ICRC, Khalid Sheikh Mohammed later described his treatment at a variety of sites, probably beginning in Afghanistan. He was stripped and held naked for a month, hog-tied and beaten, hung from the ceiling with his toes barely touching the ground, exposed to extreme cold and then doused with cold water, and in March 2003, he was waterboarded a total of 183 times. In September 2006, having experienced these and other enhanced interrogation techniques in black prisons for three and a half years, Mohammed was transferred to Guantánamo.

Who was Khalid Sheikh Mohammed, and what did US counterterrorism authorities know about him at the time of his capture? He was born in Kuwait, but his ethnic roots were in Baluchistan, a border region between Pakistan and Iran. Not yet known to hold the extremist Islamic beliefs he would later act on, he attended colleges in North Carolina, receiving a degree in mechanical engineering in 1986. Not until 1993, when it was discovered that Ramzi Yousef, the bomber of the first World Trade Center attack, was Mohammed's nephew did Mohammed come to the attention of US intelligence.

The mid-1990s saw Khalid Sheikh Mohammed in Afghanistan, where Osama bin Laden had established his headquarters and where terrorist operations on a major scale were planned. In a confession that Mohammed made after his 2006 transfer to Guantánamo, he claimed responsibility for as many as thirty-one planned or fully carried out extremist acts before a Combatant Status Review Tribunal (CSRT) conducted by the US Department of Defense.

On March 10, 2007, in broken English and with the help of an interpreter, Khalid Sheikh Mohammed testified, "I was responsible for the 9/11 Operation, from A to Z." He also claimed responsibility for the 1993 World Trade Center bombing, for the bombing of night clubs and hotels where Jewish, British,

Daniel Pearl, a *Wall Street Journal* reporter, was kidnapped by an extremist group in Pakistan in 2002. He was murdered on film.

and Australians were his targets, and for the beheading "with my blessed right hand ... of the American Jew, Daniel Pearl."

The murder of Daniel Pearl in Karachi, Pakistan, on February 1, 2002, was especially gruesome. The victim was seen speaking on camera before the act was committed. The execution was shown, and videos of the severed head were flashed around the world. Pearl, the South Asia bureau chief of the *Wall Street Journal*, had gone to Pakistan as an investigative reporter and was drawn into a trap that promised information he had been seeking about a link to al-Qaeda.

Pearl's executioner was believed to have been a member of a nationalist Pakistani movement rather than an al-Qaeda affiliate. This man, Ahmed Omar Saeed Sheikh, was apprehended and sentenced to death by hanging in July 2002 for the abduction and murder of Daniel Pearl. Khalid Sheikh Mohammed's claim in 2007 that he had personally carried out the decapitation seemed open to question, despite his statement to the CSRT that "there are pictures of me on the Internet holding his head."

In 2011, a team of students and journalists from Georgetown University released a report in which they offered up evidence that the FBI could tie Mohammed to the blade that was used to kill Pearl. What's more, an analysis of the pattern of veins in the hand of the person who is shown killing him in the video had reportedly matched Mohammed's hand. This evidence may not be permissible in court, however.

While Ahmed Omar Saeed Sheikh's lawyers do not deny that he masterminded the kidnapping of Pearl, they have argued that he was not the person to kill Pearl. In 2007, they appealed Omar's death sentence based on Mohammed's confession. In 2016, a court in Pakistan declined to hear the appeal.

Other operations that Khalid Sheikh Mohammed asserted he had planned but had not been able to carry out included the following:

- *Post–9/11 attacks on skyscrapers such as the Library Tower in California, the Sears Tower in Chicago, the Plaza Bank in the state of Washington, and the Empire State Building in New York City.*
- *Bombing and destroying the Panama Canal.*
- *The assassination of several former American presidents, including Jimmy Carter.*
- *Bombing the suspension bridges in New York.*

- *Destroying Heathrow Airport, the Canary Wharf Building, and Big Ben in the United Kingdom.*
- *Destroying the New York Stock Exchange and other financial targets after 9/11.*
- *Destroying US embassies in Indonesia, Australia, and Japan.*
- *Destroying several strategic targets in Israel, as well as El Al Israel Airlines flights and Israeli embassies in India, Azerbaijan, the Philippines, and Australia.*
- *Destroying nuclear power plants in the United States.*
- *Destroying NATO headquarters in Europe.*
- *Assassination attempts on President Clinton and Pope John Paul II while they were visiting the Philippines.*
- *The Boyinka plot to down twelve American airplanes over the Pacific.*

The number of plots against American and other targets for which Khalid Sheikh Mohammed claimed responsibility led some human rights advocates to wonder whether the harshness of his treatment at black sites and elsewhere had induced false confessions. Could the effect of being waterboarded 183 times during a concentrated period of time have contributed to Mohammed's admission of so many planned operations? Was it true that he had single-handedly surveyed, financed, and trained personnel for all those acts of destruction and assassination, or was he covering up for others? And was he so cruel and dangerous in his acts and his designs that torturing him might have been considered justifiable?

If Khalid Sheikh Mohammed was ever to be tried in a court of law in the United States, some wonder whether questions might arise about the legality of the interrogation methods used on him. If those methods were construed as torture, could their use invalidate his testimony? A trial might also pass judgment on the continuing practice of extraordinary rendition that had taken place during the Bush-Cheney administration, affecting so-called high-value suspects as well as many detainees later found to be innocent of any charges.

In reviewing Mohammed's waterboarding in 2014, the Senate Select Committee on Intelligence found that it hadn't helped US authorities capture any terrorists or thwart any terrorist plots. Rather, Mohammed apparently shared false information while he was being tortured. The highest-value information he revealed came after his torture ended, though as Dexter Filkins, writing for the *New Yorker*, points out, "This doesn't necessarily mean that torture didn't work, of course; it's possible that Mohammed was relieved that it had stopped and was grateful to his interrogators."

Torture and Trials

On April 28, 2005, during his second term in office, President Bush was asked at a White House press conference about his administration's rendition program.

"Mr. President," a reporter asked, "under the law, how would you justify the practice of renditioning, where U.S. agents who brought terror suspects abroad [take] them to a third country for interrogation? And would you stand for it if foreign agents did that to an American here?"

In keeping with a statement he made in January 2005 that "torture is never acceptable, nor do we hand over people to countries that do torture," the president replied as follows: "We operate within the law, and we send people to countries where they say they're not going to torture the people." Careful listeners to the president's response could not help wondering about the wording. Was the insertion of the phrase "where they say" the president's way of avoiding responsibility for an act that would have brought him criticism, namely, sending detainees to destinations known by the US Department of State to inflict torture on prisoners?

As President Bush's second term in office drew to a close in December 2008, Vice President Cheney was asked about the use of torture on terror suspects. "We don't do torture," he replied. "We never have. It's not something this administration subscribes to." Yet, asked whether he thought the waterboarding of Khalid Sheikh Mohammed had been appropriate, he replied, "I do."

On his first day in office in January 2009, President Barack Obama signed an executive order calling for the closing of the Guantánamo prison within one year. However, numerous difficulties arose regarding the timely transfers of the more than two hundred remaining prisoners. There were delays for other reasons, as well.

On November 13, 2009, Attorney General Eric Holder announced that Khalid Sheikh Mohammed and four alleged accomplices in the 9/11 attacks would be brought to trial. While the Bush administration had consistently argued that al-Qaeda suspects should be tried in military courts (closed to the public), the new administration felt that justice should be meted out in an open courtroom to show the world that even Khalid Sheikh Mohammed could get a fair trial in the United States.

Originally, the civilian trial was to be held in the US District Court in New York City, only blocks away from the ruins of the World Trade Center. By the end of 2010, public officials and citizens' groups were still debating the site of the trial. Some felt that the high-profile case would cause congestion and disruption and possibly even facilitate terrorist acts in Lower Manhattan.

In 2011, however, in the face of claims that a trial in a civilian court would be dangerous, among other criticisms, President Obama signed a bill that prohibited Defense Department funds from being used to transfer Guantánamo detainees to the United States. This effectively required that Mohammed and other detainees face military rather than civilian trials. The Obama administration nonetheless continued to oppose military tribunals; Obama had argued that they "failed to establish a legitimate legal framework and undermined our capability to ensure swift and certain justice."

"Khalid Sheikh Mohammed is not a common criminal, he's a war criminal," argued House Judiciary Committee Chairman Lamar Smith in 2011. "I hope the Obama administration will stop playing politics with our national security and start treating foreign terrorists like enemy combatants."

Subsequent bills signed as recently as 2019 extended the ban on the transfer of Guantánamo Bay prisoners, and as of late 2018, trial was still pending for Mohammed, who had undergone at least twenty-five pretrial hearings.

Chapter Five

LIFE AT GUANTÁNAMO

Suspects in the 9/11 attacks stood accused of one of the most heinous crimes in the history of the United States. Capturing these suspects and using their knowledge to prevent future attacks was the primary mission of antiterrorism efforts after September 11, 2001. Many argued that obtaining key information that could potentially save thousands or even tens of thousands of lives justified even the most extreme interrogation methods. At the same time, the Bush administration refused to call its methods torture. At least officially, torture was considered to be against American values.

However, in the view of numerous legal specialists and world humanitarian bodies, interrogation

Opposite: Prisoners in the war on terror, pictured wearing orange jumpsuits, are processed by military police at the Guantánamo Bay detention facility in Cuba in 2002.

methods used under the Bush administration could clearly be construed as torture. Detainees were badly beaten, waterboarded, walled, placed in stress positions, and kept in severely cramped confinement.

Other nations, among them Egypt, Jordan, and Morocco, also harbored detainees remanded to them by the United States. These governments sanction the torture of their own citizens to extract confessions. As early as September 13, 2001, President Bush was reported to have said to the ambassador from Saudi Arabia (another nation that is known to practice torture), "If we get somebody and we can't get them to cooperate, we'll hand them over to you."

The United States' own facility, Guantánamo Bay in Cuba, held more than 775 so-called enemy combatants from more than forty countries during its most active period, between January 11, 2002 and December 22, 2006. Was torture practiced on the prisoners held there without trial, 530 of whom were eventually deemed not to be terrorists and who were quietly released by the time George W. Bush left office in 2008? The use of torture is still denied by people who served in the Bush administration, including the Office of Legal Counsel and other White House lawyers. But voices from Guantánamo paint a different picture.

The Case of Adil al-Zamil

Adil al-Zamil was a Kuwaiti who worked for the Kuwait Public Authority for Housing Care. In February 2002, he was in Pakistan, where he was picked up for bounty money—between $5,000 and $10,000—and handed over to US personnel. After six weeks in the prisons of Kandahar and Bagram air bases in Afghanistan, al-Zamil was reportedly drugged, hooded, shackled, and put aboard a plane bound for Cuba.

Reports of Abuse

Visits to Guantánamo made by the International Committee of the Red Cross during 2003 indicated that the treatment of prisoners by the guards and the interrogators was unnecessarily harsh and that detainees who were not charged with crimes were being held for years before being released. The humanitarian organization lodged its complaints with the Bush administration. The response of the government, if there was one, was not made public and there was no redress.

Other sources alleged that in parts of the camp, detainees were being kept in open-air cages for extended periods as well as in solitary confinement. There were examples of some individuals lying in their own filth and of medical neglect of painful wounds and dislocated limbs.

Visitors to the prison from government agencies, such as the Federal Bureau of Investigation, reported "that the military guards were slapping prisoners, stripping them, pouring cold water over them, and making them stand until they got hypothermia."

Complaints sent to the Department of Defense by FBI agents, however, were ignored.

According to the Center for the Study of Human Rights in the Americas at the University of California at Davis, al-Zamil underwent numerous forms of torture at Guantánamo between 2002 and 2005. "While walking to the place of interrogation," al-Zamil reported, "the guards would continuously hit me on my head with sticks, and every time I [denied] their accusations [of being tied to al-Qaeda] during interrogations the guards would hit me even more, hold me high up and then fling me to the floor."

During other interrogations, al-Zamil was reportedly suspended with one hand tied to the ceiling while a gun rested on the questioner's table. Guards "used to come into my cell and force me to walk out by beating me. They used to hit me with their fists and put their feet on my head." A slamming on the head with iron handcuffs left al-Zamil with a bleeding wound that went untreated and became infected. According to the text of the Human Rights Center report at the University of California at Davis, he said that he was sexually humiliated in Guantánamo, citing an incident in which he was "stripped naked in front of women officers while they clicked photos, laughing all the time."

In a 2008 interview, al-Zamil told McClatchy Newspapers that he had been locked in a metal box without toilet facilities for about a month at Guantánamo. On another occasion, during an interrogation, he said that he cracked, telling his interrogators: "I am Osama bin Laden. Please kill me."

Al-Zamil was transferred to Kuwait in 2005, where he served out a sentence for attacking a female college student.

The Case of Moazzam Begg

Kidnapped in January 2002 from his temporary home in Pakistan and confined for a year in harsh American-run prisons in Afghanistan, Moazzam Begg, a British-born Muslim, arrived at Guantánamo in February 2003. Dazed by the tropical heat

Moazzam Begg, a former Guantánamo Bay detainee, is pictured in 2007 at the book launch for *Poems from Guantánamo: The Detainees Speak*. Begg, a British-born Muslim, was detained for three years but released without charge.

and humidity of Cuba, Begg was transferred from the airplane to the space he was to occupy for the foreseeable future. It was a windowless steel cage, covered with wire mesh that was crisscrossed to prevent looking out. A steel bed and a toilet were the only furnishings in this 6-ft by 8-ft (1.8-m by 2.4-m) space.

Begg's despair was even greater than that he had experienced in the grim confines of Kandahar and Bagram, where "each time I thought things were going to get better ... they actually got worse." Glancing around at his bare cell, he "asked for something I could use as a prayer mat, and they brought a thin camping mat, which became my mattress for the next two years." Begg later learned that the mat was known as a "suicide blanket—meaning it could not be torn up to make a noose."

The following morning, Begg was taken before a pair of interrogators who demanded that he sign a six-page confession admitting that he was a long-standing member of al-Qaeda. "The statement also claimed that I had financed a man I'd never even heard of—involved in a plot to bomb a U.S. airport in 2000—but omitted to mention how, where and when, I'd met him." Begg, who owned an Islamic bookshop in England, was also accused of operating a recruiting center for al-Qaeda.

After he signed an amended statement, denying al-Qaeda affiliations, he was returned to solitary confinement and closely watched. A year and a half later, in July 2004, Begg received visits from British intelligence officers but still had no lawyer and no Muslim chaplain as requested. In addition, his mail to and from his family was censored.

The International Red Cross paid quarterly visits to Guantánamo. "But I never thought of the Red Cross as anything more than glorified postmen—because it was only mail that they brought," Begg wrote in *Enemy Combatant*, his book about his imprisonment in Afghanistan and Cuba. Bitterly, Begg added,

"I knew that they were heavily funded by the US and therefore not as completely neutral as I had thought."

Suddenly, in October 2004, Begg found himself shackled and in blackened goggles, being moved to a communal cellblock in the main part of the camp, where he would be one of six prisoners. His cell, which resembled an outdoor dog cage, was even smaller than the previous one, and just as bare. Now, however, he had the advantage of being able to communicate through the steel mesh separations with other detainees. Neither he nor his fellow prisoners knew why the transfer had taken place.

Begg feared that despite his British citizenship, a military trial in the United States, without witnesses or a lawyer of his choice, was about to take place. In the eyes of the Bush administration, Begg was classified as an "enemy combatant" and was therefore denied the rights of a prisoner of war under the Geneva Conventions.

Unlike many of his fellow detainees, Begg had the advantages of being well-educated, speaking English as well as Arabic and Urdu, and being a citizen of the United Kingdom—an ally of the United States in the wars in Iraq and Afghanistan. Other detainees, some guilty of little more than having been in the wrong place at the wrong time, would be held without trial even beyond the years of the Bush administration.

An anxious two and a half months passed until January 2005 when, to Begg's amazement, he was visited in his cell and told that the "military has decided to hand you over to British authorities, and any charges that we had pending have been dropped." On January 25, after three years in US confinement, Begg was flown to England and returned to his home and family.

After Begg's release, he led the London-based group CAGE, which advocates for suspects of terrorism who have been denied legal rights. He was also treated for post-traumatic stress disorder.

In 2014, Begg spent seven months in Belmarsh Prison in London, England. He was being held on charges of terrorism related to two trips he had made to Syria. However, after his long imprisonment, prosecutors announced they would offer no evidence on him, and Begg was release.

Upon his release, Begg said he understood why he was imprisoned by the Americans. "I understood that they were reacting to 9/11," he told the *Guardian* newspaper. However, his imprisonment by British authorities, he argued, was "malicious" and "vindictive."

The "Twentieth Hijacker"

The attacks of September 11, 2001, had been carried out by nineteen hijackers who had taken control of four airplanes, crashing two of them into the twin towers of the World Trade Center in New York City, and one of them into the Pentagon just outside of Washington, DC. Five hijackers had been assigned to each of the three jet aircraft, and it appeared to investigators that al-Qaeda might have planned that the fourth jet, United Airlines Flight 93, would also be taken over by five hijackers.

The attack on Flight 93, however, which was believed to have been targeting the White House, involved only four hijackers. On this flight, passengers took action, causing the aircraft to crash into a field in Pennsylvania, killing all aboard.

Suspicions about the identity of the hypothetical twentieth hijacker fell on several al-Qaeda members who had been slated to enter the United States during the preceding months or were already in the country. A possible candidate was Mohammed al-Qahtani. He was a Saudi national, as had been fifteen of the nineteen hijackers, and on August 4, 2001, he had arrived on a flight from London at the international airport in Orlando, Florida.

Mohammed al-Qahtani, a Saudi national, was suspected of being the planned twentieth hijacker in the September 11, 2001, attacks. He was later held in the Guantánamo Bay prison.

Waiting to meet al-Qahtani upon his arrival was Mohammed Atta, the somber and fiercely dedicated lead hijacker of 9/11. However, al-Qahtani was refused entry into the United States by a federal immigration inspector who found him suspicious. Al-Qahtani was deported, tracked to the Middle East, and picked up in Afghanistan near the Pakistan border in December 2001.

Could al-Qahtani be the intended twentieth hijacker and, if so, might his presence on Flight 93 have allowed the hijackers to succeed in attacking the White House? What, if anything, did al-Qahtani know about the attacks? The US government believed that he might know the names of the mastermind and others involved in the plot, and thought he might be able to lead his interrogators into the very heart of the al-Qaeda operation.

Al-Qahtani arrived at Guantánamo early in 2002. The rules regarding the treatment of suspected terrorists there were still in the formative stage. Shackles, hooding, forced shaving, solitary confinement, and outdoor cages were in use. However, it was unclear how far the guards were permitted to go with regard to slapping, walling, and other bodily assaults. Was it all right to subject detainees to extremes of temperature in enclosed cells, to blast them with earsplitting music, to station snarling dogs inches from their faces, to enforce nakedness?

For the first months of al-Qahtani's confinement in Guantánamo, he offered so little information that Donald Rumsfeld, Bush's secretary of defense, advocated special interrogation techniques for the man presumed to be a would-be hijacker. Rumsfeld believed that high-value prisoners such as al-Qahtani required extreme measures.

So, beginning on August 8, 2002, al-Qahtani was held in a solitary cell flooded with blinding white light twenty-four hours a day. Loud music and temperature extremes were designed to inflict psychological trauma. Nonetheless, in November, Rumsfeld authorized longer interrogation periods, lasting as many as twenty hours per day. The secretary of defense also named sixteen additional coercive techniques that could be used on the prisoner.

The new interrogation sessions began in December 2002. At one of them, al-Qahtani was pumped full of fluid and not allowed to relieve himself until he admitted that he worked for al-Qaeda and that he had met many times with Osama bin Laden. However, when he continued to insist that he had flown to Orlando by himself and wasn't told the nature of his mission, he was refused the promised bathroom break. He then denied that he had ever met bin Laden.

Al-Qahtani's behavior grew increasing erratic. He went on hunger strikes and refused to drink water. In 2005, *Time* magazine published a detailed log covering fifty days in the life of "Detainee 063" in Guantánamo. On December 7, 2002, "a medical corpsman reports that al-Qahtani is becoming seriously dehydrated, the result of his refusing to take water regularly. He is given an intravenous hydrating drip and a doctor is summoned … but even as al-Qahtani is put under a doctor's care, [loud] music is played to 'prevent detainee from sleeping.'"

On two other occasions, the prisoner had to be transferred to a hospital because of a dangerously slow heartbeat, which was reported after he had been doused with water and then chilled to induce hypothermia. Although waterboarding was not used at Guantánamo, the "interrogators poured bottles of water on al-Qahtani's head when he refused to drink. Interrogators called this game 'Drink Water or Wear It.'"

The new coercive techniques included the use of a dog "to growl, bark, and bare his teeth at the prisoner while he was chained to the floor." At other times, al-Qahtani was led around on a leash, made to bark like a dog, and forced to perform dog tricks.

A newly authorized technique referred to as "Invasion of Space by a Female" permitted his handlers to strip him naked in front of female interrogators. Deeply shaming tactics for this man of the Muslim faith included being forced to wear a brassiere, having underwear draped over his head, and being made to dance with another male, such as an interrogator.

In his State of the Union address in January 2003, President George W. Bush informed the nation that, "[o]ne by one, the terrorists are learning the meaning of American justice." However, at around the same time, objections by the FBI and by naval officials had called a halt to the torture of al-Qahtani.

In 2005, a Pentagon inquiry into the case concluded that the methods used in al-Qahtani's interrogations were "abusive and degrading." In May 2008, a senior Pentagon official, Susan J. Crawford, dismissed military charges against the alleged twentieth hijacker. No reason for the dismissal was given at the time.

However, in January 2009, Crawford said of al-Qahtani: "His treatment met the legal definition of torture. And that's why I did not refer the case [for prosecution]." In making this statement, reports Bob Woodward of the *Washington Post*, Crawford became "the first senior Bush administration official responsible for reviewing practices at Guantánamo to publicly state that a detainee was tortured." What's more, Crawford said, the abusive techniques and coercions to which he was subjected had had a severe medical impact.

Although Crawford believed that al-Qahtani was part of the 9/11 plot, she said coerced testimony—evidence given under duress, such as during torture—should not be permissible in court. "There's no doubt in my mind he would've been on one of those planes had he gained access to the country in August 2001," Crawford said. "He's a very dangerous man. What do you do with him now if you don't charge him and try him? I would be hesitant to say 'Let him go.'"

In early 2019, ten years after President Barack Obama ordered the closure of Guantánamo, al-Qahtani remained at the prison along with thirty-nine other detainees. He had not been charged with a crime but was not recommended for transfer.

Attempts to Close Guantánamo

Since 9/11, there have been prisoners at Guantánamo Bay, Cuba, from forty-nine countries. Today, just forty of the nearly eight hundred prisoners detained there remain, but for most of these last inmates, it remains unclear when or whether they might

On January 22, 2009, President Barack Obama signs an executive order to close the Guantánamo Bay detention center. A decade later, however, the prison remains open, albeit with a dramatically reduced number of detainees.

leave. Just five have been recommended for transfer and only in the case that security conditions are met.

Interrogations under threat or administration of torture have reportedly ceased, as have acts desecrating the Quran, the holy book of Islam. Forced shaving, sexual humiliation, and other cruel and abusive treatment, too, have come to an end.

What kinds of trials await those charged with crimes? The Bush administration had advocated military tribunals, not open to the public. The Obama administration believed that military trials should be modified—that the defendant should be allowed to choose his own lawyers and that statements obtained as a result of cruel or inhuman treatment should not be permissible in court.

The Obama administration also recommended that some prisoners be tried before juries in civilian courts and with defense lawyers who could challenge the introduction of confessions that might have been based on methods of torture such as waterboarding.

In keeping with the closing of Guantánamo, the Obama administration sought to purchase an existing prison in the state of Illinois to house those Guantánamo inmates serving out their prison terms as well as those being detained indefinitely without trial. Objections immediately arose. Neither Illinois nor any other US state wanted convicted and/or suspected terrorists on its soil because of security concerns and the danger of terrorist reprisals. Supporters of the prisoner transfer, however, pointed out that Ramzi Yousef, the 1993 World Trade Center bomber, has been serving a life sentence since 1998 in a federal prison in the United States without any such consequences.

Efforts in support of housing detainees on US soil and, in tandem with this, carrying out civilian trials, fell flat in 2011 and seem unlikely to be rekindled any time soon.

Under the Obama administration, officials sought to lower the number of detainees at Guantánamo, and they succeeded; however, they encountered several obstacles along the way. Among these, there were some problems with regard to releasing those Guantánamo detainees who were not charged and were believed to be innocent. Some were not welcome in their home countries, while others—such as Chinese Muslims—were in danger of being persecuted or even executed if they returned to China. A large number of the lingering Guantánamo prisoners were from Yemen, which was becoming increasingly radicalized. It was feared that prisoners returned by the United States would be readily inducted into one of the centers of anti-American fanaticism in that nation.

A final hurdle delaying Obama's plan to close Guantánamo was opposition from Congress. Among both Republican and Democratic lawmakers there were objections not only to housing prisoners on US soil but to holding civilian trials rather than establishing military tribunals. Indignation over 9/11 still seethed among their constituents, and it was felt that judgments against the detainees should follow military procedures and principles.

Human rights and civil liberties groups, on the other hand, felt strongly that all cases should go to civilian trials in federal courts, where the validity of the evidence against a defendant could be judged on the basis of how it was obtained.

A January 30, 2018, executive order signed by President Donald Trump reversed President Obama's order to close the prison and added that future detainees may be sent there.

President Trump has not only taken a stance in support of keeping Guantánamo open, he has also expressed his support for torture. When asked in his first television interview as president whether he supported torture, President Trump told ABC News that he did. "When ISIS is doing things that nobody has ever heard of since medieval times, would I feel strongly about waterboarding? As far as I'm concerned, we have to fight fire with fire." He added that he believed that torture is effective in achieving its aims. He had pledged during a presidential debate to bring back waterboarding.

Chapter Six

THE TORTURE DEBATE TODAY

On March 13, 2018, President Donald Trump announced his nominee for director of the CIA, the United States' premier global intelligence agency. Gina Haspel had joined the CIA in 1985 and had since served in Central Europe, Turkey, and Central Asia in addition to holding two of the top three positions at the agency. However, her role in Bush-era interrogations that many considered torture sparked broad controversy surrounding whether she was fit to lead the CIA—and whether she might revive the use of torture.

In 2005, Haspel had supported the destruction of CIA video recordings that showed prisoners being waterboarded. However, this was not Haspel's only link with torture. During the Bush-era war on terror,

Opposite: Gina Haspel swears in at a confirmation hearing in 2018 to consider her nomination for the position of CIA director. Haspel previously oversaw a black site where waterboarding took place.

Haspel was responsible for overseeing a CIA black site in Thailand. During her tenure, at least one detainee was waterboarded. A 2014 report from the Senate Intelligence Committee concluded that this detainee, Abd al-Rahim al-Nashiri, offered "essentially no actionable information."

In May 2018, during her confirmation hearing before the Senate Select Committee on Intelligence, Haspel said she would not relaunch a detention and interrogation program and added, "I don't believe that torture works." However, she declined to say whether she believed that the interrogation techniques the CIA used on al-Qaeda suspects were immoral.

Congress ultimately confirmed the appointment, and Haspel became the CIA's first female director. However, her nomination had reignited the controversy over whether torture is ever an acceptable means of interrogation. Let's take a look at the arguments on both sides of the debate, then investigate how the US government and the public are reckoning with the question of torture today.

The Argument for Torture

The Bush administration always maintained its official opposition to torture, even as it had approved interrogation techniques that some considered to be torture. The Obama administration, too, opposed the use of torture. However, some argue that it is necessary in times of war. This includes President Donald Trump, who has expressed his belief that torture and waterboarding are effective and that when it comes to fighting brutal enemies such as ISIS, "we have to fight fire with fire."

English philosopher Jeremy Bentham (1748–1832) made an argument in favor of torture in some circumstances. The argument is similar to a cost–benefit analysis, weighing the gains against

English philosopher Jeremy Bentham (1748–1832) argued that torture is justifiable in some instances.

the losses. Alan M. Dershowitz describes this argument in the *Boston Globe*:

> Bentham imagined a gang of torturers who, if they remained at liberty, would torture 100 innocent victims. He then asked whether it would be moral to torture one guilty member of that gang "to make known the place" where the other torturers could be found and apprehended, and thus save 100 innocent victims from torture. His answer was yes, based on the greatest good for the greatest number.

Another argument in favor of torture insists that it is consistent with how modern warfare is waged. Sam Harris, an author and neuroscientist, condemned the Abu Ghraib abuses in a 2005 article for *Huffington Post* but argued that torture is necessary in "rare circumstances." Harris argued that, despite the likelihood that torture might produce false confessions, even the slightest possibility that it could produce useful information justifies its use on certain people:

> The bomb has been ticking ever since September 11th, 2001. Given the damage we were willing to cause to the bodies and minds of innocent children in Afghanistan and Iraq, our disavowal of torture in the case of Khalid Sheikh Mohammed seems perverse. If there is even one chance in a million that he will tell us something under torture that will lead to the further dismantling of Al Qaeda, it seems that we should use every means at our disposal to get him talking.

In his op-ed, Harris referenced the "ticking-bomb scenario," which offers the argument that torture is sometimes necessary.

A Culture of Abuse

"Let me make very clear the position of my government and our country. We do not condone torture. I have never ordered torture. I will never order torture. The values of this country are such that torture is not a part of our soul and our being."

These were the words of President George W. Bush spoken at a White House photo session on June 22, 2004, only two months after the notorious Abu Ghraib abuses. As the administration would argue, the particular abuses at Abu Ghraib had not been approved by US government officials. At the same time, other abuses, such as waterboarding, had been approved as interrogation techniques. Some argued that this created a culture in which abuse was permissible, in which interrogators felt they could adopt more and more extreme methods.

The courtroom defense of army reservist Charles A. Graner Jr. was that Graner was only following orders to "soften up" the prisoners when he committed some of the worst abuses at Abu Ghraib. Megan Ambuhl, a witness in Graner's trial who had helped take photographs of the torture at Abu Ghraib, also insisted that interrogators "encouraged us all the time" and ordered her to humiliate male prisoners. At the same time, she admitted, military intelligence officers weren't present for some of the most shocking incidents.

A 2008 investigation by the US Senate Armed Services Committee ultimately concluded that Graner and Ambuhl weren't entirely incorrect in saying they were following orders. The investigation concluded that Bush administration officials, including Donald Rumsfeld, were responsible for creating Abu Ghraib's culture of abuse because administration policies "conveyed the message that physical pressures and degradation were appropriate treatment for detainees."

As posed by the conservative columnist Charles Krauthammer, the scenario is as follows: "A terrorist has planted a nuclear bomb in New York City. It will go off in one hour. A million people will die. You capture the terrorist. He knows where it is. He's not talking.

"Question: If you have the slightest belief that hanging this man by his thumbs will get you the information, are you permitted to do it?" Krauthammer concluded that, "[n]ot only is it permissible to hang this miscreant by his thumbs. It is a moral duty."

The Argument Against Torture

Those who argue that torture is never acceptable insist that it compromises American values, violates fundamental human rights, breaks domestic and international laws, and is in fact ineffective in achieving its aims. All of these arguments can be seen in opponents' response to the ticking-bomb scenario.

To agree with Krauthammer's answer to the ticking-bomb question means to abandon principles that the United States has long lived by, opponents insist. Should policing authorities have the power to use torture on all suspected wrongdoers? How would Americans feel about foreign countries torturing US citizens captured on suspicion of crimes? They argue that using torture makes Americans more like the enemy they abhor. After all, the US government sanctioned the torture of detainees in Abu Ghraib, the very same prison in which Iraqi dictator Saddam Hussein tortured and killed his own people.

The late senator John McCain agreed that torture violates American values. Writing in 2011 for the *Washington Post*, McCain insisted:

I don't mourn the loss of any terrorist's life. What I do mourn is what we lose when by official policy or official neglect we confuse or encourage those who fight this war for us to forget that best sense of ourselves. Through the violence, chaos and heartache of war, through deprivation and cruelty and loss, we are always Americans, and different, stronger and better than those who would destroy us.

Political journalist Adam Serwer argued that fundamental moral principles, not just American ones, are compromised by torture. In a 2018 op-ed for the *Atlantic*, Serwer wrote: "The public is not served by lawlessness in those to whom it grants power over matters of life and death. The logic of the war on terror, that no act of brutality carries a cost that is too dear to pay, is one that erases all distinctions between right and wrong."

Critics of the ticking-bomb scenario also point out that it is based on the assumption that torture will produce truth. This has often failed to happen. Victims of torture falsely confess; they give unreliable information; they will say anything to obtain relief from unbearable pain. A 2014 Senate investigation confirmed that torture was an ineffective tactic in the war on terror. McCain, who was tortured as a prisoner of war, agreed that the practice simply doesn't work. "I know from personal experience that the abuse of prisoners sometimes produces good intelligence but often produces bad intelligence because under torture a person will say anything he thinks his captors want to hear—true or false—if he believes it will relieve his suffering. Often, information provided to stop the torture is deliberately misleading," McCain wrote.

McCain offered another argument against torture: that it endangers US troops. If American forces mistreat enemy

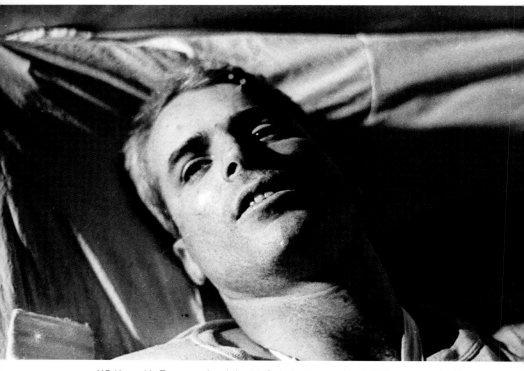

US Navy Air Force major John McCain is pictured in 1967 at a hospital in Hanoi, Vietnam. He was tortured during his time as a war prisoner.

detainees, enemy forces will be more likely to do the same to American detainees, McCain pointed out.

For more than a decade, the American Civil Liberties Union sought the release of compromising Bush-era photos that it argued provided evidence of torture committed during the war on terror. In response, the Pentagon argued that the release of such evidence of torture—though not necessarily the torture itself—would indeed endanger US troops. Terrorists or potential terrorists might use such photos as proof of American atrocities to recruit more terrorists and justify their attacks. In 2015, a federal judge ordered the Pentagon to determine, on a case-by-case basis, whether each of the estimated 1,800 photos in question would put American troops in harm's way and release those photos that would not.

Finally, opponents of torture point to the hundreds of innocent people who were tortured in the name of the war on terror. They argue that not only is this deeply unjust, it also risks radicalizing people who were not terrorists previously because those who feel they were treated unfairly by the United States might turn against the nation.

Interrogation Without Torture

Opponents of torture insist that other interrogation strategies have proven more effective. To offer an example of this, we must return to the spring of 2002. The CIA had just captured Abu Zubaydah, its first presumed high-level detainee, perhaps close to the command of Osama bin Laden. The circumstances of Zubaydah's capture, which took place in Faisalabad, Pakistan, had been violent. At the time of his transfer to the CIA black site in Thailand, where he would be held for four years, he was impaired by serious wounds and had bullet fragments in his stomach, groin, and leg.

In the early days after the attacks of September 11, 2001, the FBI was involved in the interrogation of CIA prisoners. A principal investigator in Zubaydah's case was an FBI agent born in Lebanon: Ali Soufan. He spoke Arabic and was an instructor for other interrogators. In the FBI's initial approach to Zubaydah, Soufan stated, "We kept him alive. It wasn't easy, he couldn't drink, he had a fever. I was holding ice to his lips."

Soufan tried to learn as much as he could about Zubaydah's background. He nursed his wounds, found out his family nickname, and gradually gained his confidence. When he showed Zubaydah photographs of terror suspects, Zubaydah identified Khalid Sheikh Mohammed as having been the mastermind of 9/11.

As early as three months before the "torture memo" of August 1, 2002, Soufan had been horrified to come upon Zubaydah stripped nude and being bombarded with loud music in a room in which the temperature had been reduced to near freezing. He also discovered a dark, wooden, coffin-like box built for Zubaydah in which the prisoner could be confined indefinitely.

"We're the United States of America, and we don't do that kind of thing," Soufan shouted at the CIA official who was responsible. The official retorted that he had gotten approval from the "highest levels" in Washington and told Soufan that further authorization was coming from the Justice Department. The harsh techniques, Soufan was told, were justified because previous methods were not working.

On April 22, 2009, in an opinion piece in the *New York Times*, Soufan recalled that time. "It is inaccurate, however, to say that Abu Zubaydah had been uncooperative," he wrote. "I questioned him from March to June 2002 … Under traditional interrogation methods, he provided us with important actionable intelligence. We discovered, for example, that Khalid Sheikh Mohammed was the mastermind of the 9/11 attacks."

Soufan notified then–FBI director Robert Mueller of the cruel treatment being applied by CIA officials and especially by the inexperienced contractors the CIA had hired for the purpose. Mueller, however, ordered Soufan and another FBI agent home and barred FBI agents from further participation in CIA interrogations.

Soufan wrote in the *New York Times*: "One of the worst consequences of the use of these harsh techniques was that it reintroduced the so-called Chinese wall between the C.I.A. and the F.B.I., similar to the communications obstacles that prevented us from working together to stop the 9/11 attacks." That is, the two agencies were no longer sharing information and collaborating in the war on terror—or, at least, such sharing was limited. While Soufan agreed that the CIA was essential to the national security of the United States, he abhorred the use of torture versus "intelligent" intelligence-gathering.

The FBI also took part in interrogations at Guantánamo in the early months of 2002 and reported more than two dozen cases of alarming abuse. "On a couple of occasions," an FBI agent wrote to headquarters, "I entered interview rooms to find a detainee chained hand and foot in a fetal position on the floor, with no chair, food or water. Most times they urinated or defecated on themselves, and had been left there for 18–24 hours or more."

Other examples of abuse witnessed by FBI agents "included wrapping a prisoner's head in duct tape for chanting the Koran, dressing a soldier as a Catholic priest and pretending to 'baptize' a Muslim prisoner, and draping an Israeli flag over an Arab prisoner."

Defense Secretary Rumsfeld, however, fired the general who originally headed the Guantánamo facility for being too soft on the detainees and for calling to account prison guards who had behaved harshly. In November 2002, Rumsfeld replaced him with Major General Geoffrey Miller, who later went on to advise the administrators of Abu Ghraib in the use of cruel and degrading treatment.

As in the case of Zubaydah, FBI agents were withdrawn from Guantánamo by the agency's director, Robert Mueller. It was perhaps his justification that, while the war on terror raged, it would have been unseemly for one government surveillance agency, the FBI, to declare war on another, the CIA.

Shifting Perspectives on Torture

During the first term of the Bush administration, support for its program of incarceration of detainees at home and abroad, and of enhanced interrogation techniques, ran high. The public also supported the war in Afghanistan, as that nation was then reported to be the home base of Osama bin Laden. A major segment of the press and the public also favored the 2003 invasion of Iraq, which as time passed was shown to have been based on false information. Iraq did not have arsenals of chemical and biological weapons; it was not in the process of developing nuclear weapons; and it was not closely tied to bin Laden and his al-Qaeda network.

With the invasion of Iraq by the United States came the scandal at Abu Ghraib prison. Secretary of Defense Donald Rumsfeld who, along with Vice President Dick Cheney, was a strong advocate of the torture policy and its major architect, learned of the abuses in January 2004. However, he reportedly sat on the information for months, until its disclosure in the public media in April. When the photographic evidence surfaced, Rumsfeld first remarked that he was surprised to learn that there were cameras in the prison camp. Almost a year later, on February 6, 2005, Rumsfeld told television interviewer George Stephanopoulos on *ABC This Week* that "what was going on in the midnight shift in Abu Ghraib prison halfway across the world is something that clearly someone in Washington, D.C. can't manage or deal with."

George W. Bush was elected to a second term in November 2004. In his campaign, the president insisted that a successful war on terror could be waged only by his team. He declared that his policies had kept America safe from further attacks and would continue to do so for four more years.

However, with the election of President Barack Obama in November 2008, White House policy on torture, the US military presence in Afghanistan and Iraq, and the treatment of prisoners in the war on terror changed dramatically. President Obama sought in the early days of his administration to express his strong disapproval of the policies and practices of his predecessors. Speaking to the United Nations General Assembly on September 23, 2009, the president said, "For those who question the character and cause of my nation, I ask you to look at the concrete actions we have taken in just nine months. On my first day in office I prohibited—without exception or equivocation—the use of torture by the United States of America."

Meanwhile, members of the Bush team continued to assert that the interrogation techniques used on prisoners both at Guantánamo and abroad had been acceptable. Speaking at the National Press Club in June 2009, former vice president Dick Cheney defended these enhanced interrogation practices. Referring to the torture memo of 2002, Cheney asserted, "We all approved it. I'm a strong believer in it. I think it was the right thing to do."

Assigning Responsibility

Even as some have firmly held that waterboarding was a necessary interrogation tool in the war on terror, others have insisted that the Bush administration ignored or broke domestic and international law. Many legal authorities have asserted that the Constitution of the United States was and continues to be violated in that detainees have been denied the "due process of law" and have been subjected to "unreasonable searches and seizures" and "cruel and unusual punishment." The Uniform Code of Military Justice, which specifies the punishments for torture-related crimes by the

US military worldwide, was sidestepped in implementing these interrogation methods.

The Geneva Conventions covering the treatment of prisoners of war throughout the world were effectively ignored, human rights advocates have argued, as was the 1994 United Nations Convention against Torture and Other Cruel, Inhuman or Degrading Treatment or Punishment. This latter convention defines torture as follows:

> *Torture means any act by which severe pain or suffering, whether physical or mental, is intentionally inflicted on a person for such purposes as obtaining from him or a third person information or a confession, punishing him for an act he or a third person has committed or is suspected of having committed, or intimidating or coercing him or a third person, or for any reason based on discrimination of any kind, when such pain or suffering is inflicted by or at the instigation of or with the consent or acquiescence of a public official or other person acting in an official capacity. It does not include pain or suffering arising only from, inherent in or incidental to lawful sanctions.*

If the Obama administration were to have investigated the Bush administration for war crimes as a result of its torture policies, where would it have started? At which level of government would an examining body, such as a truth commission, be aimed?

While the former president, vice president, and secretary of defense had authorized many of the questionable interrogation techniques, also prominent in the line of direct responsibility for the implementation of torture in the prisons at home and abroad were military and CIA commanders, as well as agents and interrogators. They were for the most part poorly trained

John Yoo, a coauthor of the so-called torture memos, testifies on Capitol Hill on June 26, 2008.

for their jobs, as revealed at Abu Ghraib. Many were ignorant of the religion and culture of the prisoners and did not speak their language. Yet, for the Obama administration to undertake a wide-ranging investigation of America's secret intelligence agency or of its military-command structure was risky in terms of national security.

Even as Senator John McCain condemned the practices of the Bush administration as torture, he argued in 2011 that putting offenders on trial wasn't the right approach. "I don't believe anyone should be prosecuted for having used these techniques, and I agree that the administration should state definitively that they won't be," McCain wrote.

Another potential target for investigation of the previous administration was the Office of Legal Counsel (OLC) as well as other White House lawyers. This group, including John Yoo and Jay Bybee, was closely associated with Vice President Cheney and had authored the torture memos.

Yoo defended his actions in the *Los Angeles Times* in July 2004: "We did not take a policy position. All we did was give advice, as lawyers do, on what would be a defense if you got into trouble." The lawyers had not directly ordered the torture of prisoners; they had simply put forward a definition of torture with the goal of ensuring the legality of specific interrogation practices.

Apparently fearing condemnation of the OLC for justifying waterboarding and other enhanced interrogation techniques, the Department of Justice started an internal investigation in 2005, during Bush's second term in office, to determine whether Yoo and Bybee had been guilty of "professional misconduct" or "reckless disregard."

In February 2010, after five years of deliberation, the Justice Department of the Obama administration decided that the two lawyers were not guilty as charged. By 2010, Yoo had returned

President Donald Trump, pictured here in 2017, has expressed his belief that torture is effective and promised to bring back waterboarding.

to teaching law at the University of California at Berkeley and Bybee had been given a lifetime appointment as a federal judge.

Looking Ahead

Donald Trump has taken a stronger stance in support of torture than either of his predecessors, pledging during the presidential campaign to bring back waterboarding and a "hell of a lot worse." Trump has argued that "torture works"—that is, that it succeeds in obtaining pivotal information—despite a 2014 report from the US Senate Select Committee on Intelligence concluding that torture in the war on terror was not effective. However, Trump has added, even "if it doesn't work, they deserve it anyway."

Early in his administration, President Trump seems to have considered reviving the use of torture and reauthorizing the CIA's use of black sites. In January 2017, the draft of an executive order titled "Detention and Interrogation of Enemy Combatants" was leaked to the press.

This draft aimed to revoke a 2009 executive order by President Obama that banned CIA black sites. It would have also revived a 2007 executive order by President Bush, later shot down by Obama, that sought to exempt some torture or advanced-interrogation techniques from being considered war crimes under the internationally ratified Geneva Conventions. Finally, the Trump administration's draft executive order would have revoked the International Committee of the Red Cross's access to detainees in US custody—access which in the past has helped to reveal instances of torture and the poor treatment of prisoners.

However, the draft executive order met with strong criticism in some camps. The order was "flirting with a return to the 'enhanced interrogation program' and the environment that gave rise to it," said Elisa Massimino, director of Human Rights First. Massimino also pointed out that many retired military personnel and leaders have called torture "illegal, immoral and damaging to national security."

By February, in the face of widespread criticism, the Trump administration removed text from the order that related to torture and black sites.

Whether future US policies will revive interrogation techniques that amount to torture is unclear. Torture remains illegal under international law, but US presidents have chosen to ignore international law and agreements before and are likely to again. Meanwhile, the debate over what amounts to torture, and whether torture is ever justified, may continue for many years to come.

Glossary

aristocracy A group of upper-class, wealthy, or high-ranking individuals.

autocracy A system of government in which one person possesses all the power.

black site A location where a highly classified defense or military project is taking place.

burka A loose garment covering the face and body worn by some women of the Muslim faith.

classified Secret.

court-martial To put a member of the armed forces on trial before a court of commissioned officers and/or other military personnel.

cryptonym A code name.

defecate To discharge feces.

due process Fair treatment through access to a trial and/or other means of defending oneself.

enhanced interrogation Another term for what many believe to be torture.

executive order A rule issued by an executive authority, such as the US president, that has the force of law.

extradite To deliver a prisoner to the custody of another state for prosecution.

extraordinary rendition The transfer of a suspected terrorist to another country for the purposes of interrogating and imprisoning him or her without the normally required legal processes.

habeas corpus A legal means of reporting unlawful imprisonment to a court so that the court can determine whether such detention is lawful.

heresy A belief or opinion contrary to what is officially sanctioned by a religious organization.

hypothermia Below-normal body temperature.

Islam The religious faith of Muslims, which includes the belief in a single god, Allah, and the prophet Muhammad.

martyrdom Dying for the sake of a cause or one's religious faith.

monarchy Absolute rule by a single person.

Muslim An adherent of the Islamic faith.

proletariat The laboring class; the lowest socioeconomic class.

waterboarding A form of enhanced interrogation that simulates drowning; many argue that it is a form of torture.

wiretap To gain access to a phone line or signal in order to listen in and gather information.

Further Information

Books

Innes, Brian, and Manny Gomez. *The History of Torture* (Crime and Detection). London: Amber Books Ltd., 2017.

McCain, John, and Mark Salter. *The Restless Wave: Good Times, Just Causes, Great Fights, and Other Appreciations*. New York: Simon & Schuster, 2018.

Senate Select Committee on Intelligence and Dianne Feinstein. *The Senate Intelligence Committee Report on Torture: Committee Study of the Central Intelligence Agency's Detention and Interrogation Program*. New York: Melville House, 2014.

Steffens, Bradley. *Torture* (Human Rights in Focus). San Diego, CA: ReferencePoint Press, 2017.

Websites

Association for the Prevention of Torture
https://www.apt.ch
This organization, founded in 1977, advocates transparency in matters of torture and opposes torture as "one of the most serious violations of a person's fundamental rights." It has supported regional and international antitorture treaties.

Convention Against Torture: United Nations Treaty Collection
https://treaties.un.org/pages/ViewDetails.aspx?src=IND&mtdsg_no=IV-9&chapter=4&lang=en

On this website, read the text of the 1984 international Convention Against Torture and Other Cruel, Inhuman or Degrading Treatment or Punishment and learn what countries signed it and when.

International Committee of the Red Cross (ICRC)

https://www.icrc.org

Founded in 1863, the International Committee of the Red Cross is the oldest private humanitarian organization. Its chief concerns are the fair and humane treatment of prisoners of war and other enemy detainees, refugees, and civilian disaster victims.

Videos

Facts on Torture

https://www.humanrightsfirst.org/campaigns/never-torture/facts-torture

This series of videos lays out a variety of arguments against the use of torture through interviews with trained interrogators.

Foreign Policy Explained, Ep. 3: Torture & Police Brutality in America by the Government

https://www.youtube.com/watch?v=JY8uMYHXXsw

This video takes a look at moments in the history of the United States when US citizens were subjected to torture.

How Americans Really Feel About Torture

https://www.msnbc.com/up/watch/how-americans-really-feel-about-torture-371737667887

This report explains how Americans' opinions on whether torture is justified have changed over the years.

Organizations

Amnesty International

1 Easton Street
London, WC1X 0DW
United Kingdom
+44 20 74135500
http://www.amnesty.org

Amnesty International (AI) is a nongovernmental organization (NGO) that operates worldwide to end human rights violations, including torture, genocide, and the death penalty.

Canadian Centre for International Justice

312 Laurier Avenue East
Ottawa, ON K1N 1H9
Canada
(613) 230-6114
https://www.ccij.ca

This organization works to help survivors of torture and genocide find justice on the international stage.

Correctional Service of Canada

National Headquarters
340 Laurier Avenue West
Ottawa, ON K1A 0P9
Canada
(613) 992-5891
https://www.canada.ca/en/correctional-service.html

This agency of the Canadian federal government is tasked with administering prison sentences and managing detention facilities.

European Court of Human Rights

Council of Europe

F-67075 Strasbourg cedex

France

+33 (0)3 88 41 20 18

http://echr.coe.int

European Court of Human Rights (Cour européenne des droits de l'homme, or ECtHR) has dealt with abuses by the Soviet Union and by post-Soviet Russia, by the United Kingdom in its treatment of Irish prisoners, and with other infractions committed by its European members.

Human Rights Watch

350 Fifth Avenue, 34th Floor

New York, NY 10118

(212) 290-4700

http://www.hrw.org

Human Rights Watch is a leading nongovernmental organization that promotes human rights on an international scale. It works to document and prevent torture, genocide, capital punishment, and child labor, among other causes.

US Department of Justice

950 Pennsylvania Avenue NW

Washington, DC 20530-0001

(202) 353-1555

http://justice.gov

This department of the federal government is responsible for upholding the law and seeking "just punishment for those guilty of unlawful behavior."

Bibliography

Ackerman, Spencer. "Judge Criticizes Pentagon Suppression of Hundreds of Bush-Era Torture Photos." *Guardian* (UK), May 11, 2016. https://www.theguardian.com/us-news/2016/may/11/pentagon-military-torture-photos-george-w-bush-war-on-terror.

———. "Qaeda Killer's Veins Implicate Him in Journo's Murder." *WIRED*, January 20, 2011. https://www.wired.com/2011/01/qaeda-killers-veins-implicate-him-in-journos-murder.

"A Legal Definition of Torture." Association for the Prevention of Torture. Accessed January 3, 2019. https://www.apt.ch/en/what-is-torture.

"Amnesty International Letter to Secretary of Defense Rumsfeld." Torturing Democracy, January 7, 2002. https://nsarchive2.gwu.edu/torturingdemocracy/documents/20020107.pdf.

Associated Press in Warsaw. "Poland Pays $250,000 to Victims of CIA Rendition and Torture." *Guardian* (UK), May 15, 2015. https://www.theguardian.com/world/2015/may/15/poland-pays-250000-alleged-victims-cia-rendition-torture.

Begg, Moazzem, with Victoria Brittain. *Enemy Combatant: My Imprisonment at Guantánamo, Bagram, and Kandahar.* New York: New Press, 2006.

"Bush: Don't Wait for Mushroom Cloud." CNN, October 8, 2002. http://edition.cnn.com/2002/ALLPOLITICS/10/07/bush.transcript.

CNN Library. "CIA Torture Report Fast Facts." CNN, September 26, 2018. https://www.cnn.com/2015/01/29/us/cia-torture-report-fast-facts/index.html.

Cobain, Ian, and Randeep Ramesh. "Moazzam Begg Complains of 'Malicious' and 'Vindictive' Detention." *Guardian* (UK), October 3, 2014. https://www.theguardian.com/world/2014/oct/03/moazzam-begg-malicious-vindictive-detainment.

"Commander in Chief Lands on USS Lincoln." CNN, May 2, 2003. http://www.cnn.com/2003/ALLPOLITICS/05/01/bush.carrier.landing.

"Daniel Pearl Case: SHC Judge Declines to Hear Omar Saeed Sheikh's Appeal." *Express Tribune* (Pakistan), April 27, 2016. https://tribune.com.pk/story/1092205/daniel-pearl-case-shc-judge-declines-to-hear-omar-saeed-sheikhs-appeal.

Danner, Chas. "White House Backing Down on Renewed Use of Torture, Black Sites." *New York Magazine*, February 4, 2017. http://nymag.com/intelligencer/2017/02/white-house-backing-down-on-revival-of-torture-black-sites.html.

Danner, Mark. "Tales from Torture's Dark World." *New York Times*, March 14, 2009. https://www.nytimes.com/2009/03/15/opinion/15danner.html.

———. *Torture and Truth: America, Abu Ghraib, and the War on Terror.* New York: New York Review Books, 2004.

"Deputy Secretary of Defense Wolfowitz Interview on the
Pentagon Channel." US Department of Defense, May 4,
2004. http://archive.defense.gov/Transcripts/Transcript.
aspx?TranscriptID=2970.

Dershowitz, Alan M. "A Choice of Evils." *Boston Globe*, September
18, 2014. https://www.bostonglobe.com/opinion/2014/09/17/
torture-tool-fight-against-terrorist-groups-like-
isis/1Tfqfk1Amck7Rh9kEra8IN/story.html.

El Gamal, Rania. "Kuwaiti Gitmo Detainees Speak Out About Abuse."
Kuwait Times, December 1, 2006. http://humanrights.ucdavis.
edu/projects/the-Guantanamo-testimonials-project/testimonies/
prisoner-testimonies/kuwaiti-gitmo-detainees-speak-out-about-
abuse.

Farina, Christine. "A Review of 'Torture Through the Ages.'" *Journal
of Criminal Justice and Popular Culture*, 9 (2001): 31–32.

Fenton, Jenifer. "Life After Guantanamo Bay." Al Jazeera,
March 22, 2012. https://www.aljazeera.com/indepth/
features/2012/03/2012322135213659138.html.

Filkins, Dexter. "Khalid Sheikh Mohammed and the C.I.A." *New
Yorker*, December 31, 2014. https://www.newyorker.com/news/
news-desk/khalid-sheikh-mohammed-cia.

Fletcher, Laurel E., Eric Stover, et al. "Guantánamo and Its
Aftermath: U.S. Detention and Interrogation Practices and
Their Impact on Former Detainees." Human Rights Center,
International Human Rights Law Clinic, Center for Constitutional
Rights, November 2008. http://hrlibrary.umn.edu/OathBetrayed/
Gtmo-Aftermath.pdf.

Foster, Caitlin. "These Photos Show 17 Years of the US-Led 'Forever War' in Afghanistan as the Conflict Becomes Deadlier Than Ever." *Business Insider*, October 27, 2018. https://www. businessinsider.com/photos-from-17-years-of-the-us-led- forever-war-in-afghanistan-2018-10.

Gellman, Barton. *Angler: The Cheney Vice-Presidency*. New York: Penguin, 2008.

Glaberson, William. "Detainee Was Tortured, a Bush Official Confirms." *New York Times*, January 14, 2009. https://www. nytimes.com/2009/01/14/us/14gitmo.html.

Glass, Andrew. "Bush Announces Launch of Operation Iraqi Freedom, March 19, 2003." *POLITICO*, March 18, 2017. https:// www.politico.com/story/2017/03/bush-announces-launch-of- operation-iraqi-freedom-march-19-2003-236134.

Goldman, Adam. "Gina Haspel, Trump's Choice for C.I.A., Played Role in Torture Program." *New York Times*, March 18, 2018. https://www.nytimes.com/2018/03/13/us/politics/gina-haspel- cia-director-nominee-trump-torture-waterboarding.html.

Goldman, Adam, and Kathy Gannon. "Death Shed Light on CIA 'Salt Pit' near Kabul." Associated Press, March 28, 2010. http:// www.nbcnews.com/id/36071994/ns/us_news-security/t/death- shed-light-cia-salt-pit-near-kabul/#.XCq0WS3MyDU.

Goldstein, Sarah. "Wrongly Held, Never Tried, Fighting Back." *Nation*, December 26, 2005. https://www.thenation.com/article/ wrongly-held-never-tried-fighting-back.

Gourevitch, Philip, and Errol Morris. *The Ballad of Abu Ghraib*. New York, Penguin, 2009.

Grey, Stephen. *Ghost Plane: The True Story of the CIA Rendition and Torture Program*. New York: St. Martin's Griffin, 2007.

"The Guantánamo Docket." *New York Times*. Accessed December 31, 2018. https://www.nytimes.com/interactive/projects/ Guantánamo/detainees/10016-abu-zubaydah.

Harris, Sam. "In Defense of Torture." *HuffPost*, October 17, 2005. https://www.huffingtonpost.com/sam-harris/in-defense-of-torture_b_8993.html.

Hawkins, John. "RWN's Favorite George W. Bush Quotes." Right Wing News, March 20, 2012. https://rightwingnews.com/ quotes/rwns-favorite-george-w-bush-quotes-2.

Hersh, Seymour M. *Chain of Command: The Road from 9/11 to Abu Ghraib*. New York: HarperCollins, 2004.

Isikoff, Michael. "We Could Have Done This the Right Way." *Newsweek*, May 4, 2009.

Kane, Paul, and Joby Warrick. "Cheney Led Briefings of Lawmakers to Defend Interrogation Techniques." *Washington Post*, June 3, 2009.

Kerrigan, Michael. *The Instruments of Torture*. Guilford, CT: The Lyons Press, Globe Pequot, 2007.

Landler, Mark, Helene Cooper, and Eric Schmitt. "Trump Withdraws U.S. Forces from Syria, Declaring 'We Have Won Against ISIS.'" *New York Times*, December 19, 2018. https://www.nytimes.com/2018/12/19/us/politics/trump-syria-turkey-troop-withdrawal.html.

Lasseter, Tom. "Guantánamo Inmate Database: Adel Al Zamel." McClatchy Newspapers, 2008. https://web.archive.org/web/20080620105846/http://detainees.mcclatchydc.com/detainees/60.

"Leading by Example? Torture Ten Years after 9/11." *Human Rights*, American Bar Association, March 7, 2012. https://www.americanbar.org/publications/human_rights_magazine_home/human_rights_vol38_2011/human_rights_winter2011/leading_by_example_torture_ten_years_after_9-11.

Mashal, Mujib. "C.I.A.'s Afghan Forces Leave a Trail of Abuse and Anger." *New York Times*, December 31, 2018. https://www.nytimes.com/2018/12/31/world/asia/cia-afghanistan-strike-force.html?action=click&module=Top%20Stories&pgtype=Homepage.

Mayer, Jane. *The Dark Side: The Inside Story of How the War on Terror Turned into a War on American Ideals*. New York: Anchor Books, 2009.

McCain, John. "Bin Laden's Death and the Debate over Torture." *Washington Post*, May 11, 2011. https://www.washingtonpost.com/opinions/bin-ladens-death-and-the-debate-over-torture/2011/05/11/AFd1mdsG_story.html?utm_term=.dcd7e6faf9f3.

Meyer, Dick. "Rush: MPs Just 'Blowing Off Steam.'" CBS News,
May 16, 2004. https://www.cbsnews.com/news/rush-mps-just-
blowing-off-steam.

Miller, John. "Interview with Osama bin Laden." ABC News, May 28,
1998.

Mindock, Clark. "Lithuania and Romania Fined for Complying with
CIA Torture, European Court Rules." *Independent* (UK), May 31,
2018. https://www.independent.co.uk/news/world/americas/
cia-torture-romania-lithuania-europe-court-human-rights-abu-
zubaydah-abd-alrahim-alnashiri-a8378236.html.

Myre, Greg. "CIA Nominee Gina Haspel Faced Tough Questioning at
Her Confirmation Hearing." NPR, May 9, 2018. https://www.npr.
org/2018/05/09/609851202/cia-nominee-gina-haspel-faced-
tough-questioning-at-her-confirmation-hearing.

Peters, Edward. *Torture*. Philadelphia: University of Pennsylvania
Press, Expanded Edition, 1996.

Pilkington, Ed. "I Think We've Done Pretty Well." *Guardian* (UK),
December 17, 2008.

"President Bush Welcomes Prime Minister of Hungary." White
House, President George W. Bush Archives, June 22, 2004.
https://georgewbush-whitehouse.archives.gov/news/
releases/2004/06/20040622-4.html.

Pyle, Christopher H. *Getting Away with Torture: Secret Government,
War Crimes, and the Rule of Law*. Washington, DC: Potomac
Books, 2009.

"Q&A: Guantanamo Bay, US Detentions, and the Trump Administration." Human Rights Watch, June 27, 2018. https://www.hrw.org/news/2018/06/27/qa-Guantánamo-bay-us-detentions-and-trump-administration#q9.

"Redefining Torture?" *Frontline*, October 18, 2005. https://www.pbs.org/wgbh/pages/frontline/torture/themes/redefining.html.

Ryan, Jason, and Huma Khan. "In Reversal, Obama Orders Guantanamo Military Trial for 9/11 Mastermind Khalid Sheikh Mohammed." ABC News, April 4, 2011. https://abcnews.go.com/Politics/911-mastermind-khalid-sheikh-mohammed-military-commission/story?id=13291750.

Savage, Charlie. "Trump Poised to Lift Ban on C.I.A. 'Black Site' Prisons." *New York Times*, January 25, 2017. https://www.nytimes.com/2017/01/25/us/politics/cia-detainee-prisons.html.

"Senate Approves Iraq War Resolution." CNN, October 11, 2002. http://edition.cnn.com/2002/ALLPOLITICS/10/11/iraq.us.

Serwer, Adam. "Obama's Legacy of Impunity for Torture." *Atlantic*, March 14, 2018. https://www.theatlantic.com/politics/archive/2018/03/obamas-legacy-of-impunity-for-torture/555578.

Shah, Imtiaz. "Pearl Murder Convict to Appeal after Confession." Reuters, March 19, 2007. https://www.reuters.com/article/us-pakistan-pearl/pearl-murder-convict-to-appeal-after-confession-idUSISL18520070319.

Shane, Scott. "Divisions Arose on Rough Tactics for Qaeda Figure." *New York Times*, April 17, 2009. https://www.nytimes.com/2009/04/18/world/middleeast/18zubaydah.html.

———. "Torture Versus War." *New York Times*, April 19, 2009. https://www.nytimes.com/2009/04/19/weekinreview/19shane.html.

Singh, Amrit. "European Court of Human Rights Finds Against CIA Abuse of Khaled El-Masri." *Guardian* (UK), December 13, 2012. https://www.theguardian.com/commentisfree/2012/dec/13/european-court-human-rights-cia-abuse-khaled-elmasri.

Soufan, Ali. "My Tortured Decision." *New York Times*, April 22, 2009. https://www.nytimes.com/2009/04/23/opinion/23soufan.html.

Suskind, Ron. *The One Percent Doctrine: Deep Inside America's Pursuit of Its Enemies Since 9/11*. New York: Simon & Schuster, 2006.

Synovitz, Ron. "Icons of the Iraq War: Abu Ghraib's Lynndie England and Prisoner Abuse." Radio Free Europe/Radio Liberty, March 17, 2013. https://www.rferl.org/a/iraq-war-lynndie-ghraib/24930947.html.

"Syria Conflict: Trump Slows down Troop Withdrawal." BBC News, December 31, 2018. https://www.bbc.com/news/world-us-canada-46723603.

Tenet, George, and Bill Harlow. *At the Center of the Storm: My Years at the CIA*. New York: HarperCollins, 2007.

"Torturing Democracy." Accessed January 4, 2018. https://nsarchive2.gwu.edu/torturingdemocracy/index.html.

"Trump: 'Waterboarding Absolutely Works.'" BBC News, January 25, 2017. https://www.bbc.com/news/av/world-us-canada-38751516/donald-trump-waterboarding-absolutely-works.

Weisman, Steven R. "Powell Calls His U.N. Speech a Lasting Blot on His Record." *New York Times*, September 9, 2005. https://www.nytimes.com/2005/09/09/politics/powell-calls-his-un-speech-a-lasting-blot-on-his-record.html.

Woodward, Bob. "Guantanamo Detainee Was Tortured, Says Official Overseeing Military Trials." *Washington Post*, January 14, 2009. http://www.washingtonpost.com/wp-dyn/content/article/2009/01/13/AR2009011303372.html.

———. *State of Denial: Bush at War, Part III*. New York: Simon & Schuster, 2006.

Yoo, John C. "A Crucial Look at Torture Law." *Los Angeles Times*, July 6, 2004.

Zagorin, Adam, and Michael Duffy. "Inside the Interrogation of Detainee 063." *Time*, June 19, 2005. http://time.com/3624326/inside-the-interrogation-of-detainee-063.

Zengerle, Patricia. "Obama to Sign Defense Bill with Guantanamo Restrictions." Reuters, November 10, 2015. https://www.reuters.com/article/us-usa-defense-congress/obama-to-sign-defense-bill-with-Guantanamo-restrictions-idUSKCN0SZ27H20151110.

Zernike, Kate. "Army Reservist's Defense Rests in Abu Ghraib Abuse Case." *New York Times*, January 14, 2005. https://www.nytimes.com/2005/01/14/us/army-reservists-defense-rests-in-abu-ghraib-abuse-case.html.

Index

Page numbers in **boldface** refer to images.

About the Authors

Erin L. McCoy is a literature, language, and cultural studies educator and an award-winning photojournalist and poet. She holds a master of arts degree in Hispanic studies and a master of fine arts degree in creative writing from the University of Washington. She has edited more than two dozen nonfiction books for young adults, including *The Mexican-American War*, *The Israel-Palestine Border Conflict*, and *Poverty: Public Crisis or Private Struggle?* from Cavendish Square Publishing. She is from Louisville, Kentucky.

Lila Perl published more than sixty books for young people and adults, including fiction and nonfiction. Her nonfiction writings were mainly in the fields of social history, family memoir, and biography. Two of her books were honored with American Library Association Notable awards. Ten titles were selected as Notable Children's Trade Books in the Field of Social Studies. Lila Perl also received a Boston Globe Horn Book Award, a Sidney Taylor Committee Award, and a Young Adults' Choice Award from the International Reading Association. The New York Public Library has cited her work among Best Books for the Teen Age.